TURDLE

Solve the cr*p out of these lavatorial logic puzzles

IVANNA DUMP

First published in Great Britain in 2024 by White Ladder
An imprint of Hodder & Stoughton Limited
An Hachette UK company

1

A CIP catalogue record for this title is available from the British Library

Paperback ISBN 9781399738651

Typeset in Plantin Std by seagulls.net

Printed and bound in Great Britain by Clays Ltd, Elcograf S.p.A.

Hodder & Stoughton Limited
Carmelite House
50 Victoria Embankment
London EC4Y 0DZ

www.hodder.co.uk

CONTENTS

INTRODUCTION

Welcome to the case files of Inspector Poupe, the world's leading faecal detective. Confident of his unrivalled talent for sniffing out the poopetrators of manure-based misdemeanours, he has exclusively shared with us 60 of his smelliest cases. Do you have what it takes to be a crap detective?

To help you out, Inspector Poupe has graciously shared his ingenious method for cracking cases. While some detectives might let the clues stew in their head like a blocked toilet, Inspector Poupe has created a grid which allows him to quickly cross-reference the facts of the case. This cunning trick allows him to logically follow through on his deductions and swiftly get to the bottom of any mystery. Here's an example grid:

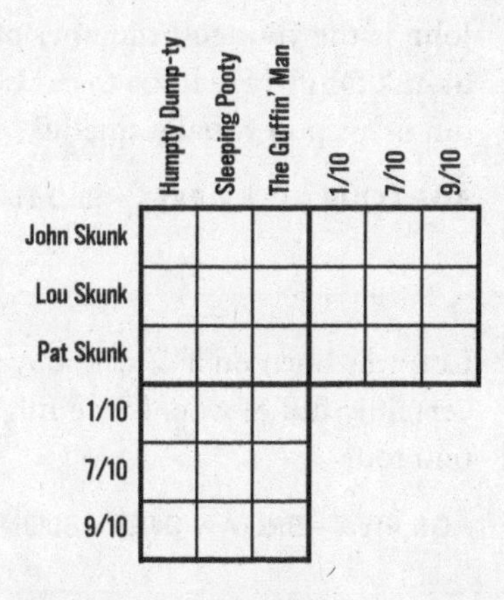

Each puzzle starts by presenting you with the details of a case, and notes on each of the categories. For this example puzzle, the case is called **'The Weakest Stink'**, and the scenario is as follows:

The Skunk family pride themselves on living up to their name by doing extremely smelly poos. They have recently patented a

SmellScale™ that they believe is an objective way of measuring the smelliness of any given poo.

Today they've been benchmarking their kids against the scale in a blind sniff test. They're devastated to discover that one of them has poo that barely registers on the SmellScale™ at all, and could dishonour the family name.

Inspector Poupe is summoned immediately. He soon manages to link each suspect to their favourite nursery rhyme and smelliness score to help the Skunks identify the 'culprit'.

The description of each case is followed by information about the suspects and other categories:

CATEGORY 1: SUSPECTS

John Skunk

John is the youngest member of the Skunk family. He loves to eat boiled eggs, but is his poo equally smelly?

AGE FOUR – BLUE EYES – RED HAIR

Lou Skunk

Lou was born on a Wednesday and is certainly full of woe. Is she full of smelly poo too?

AGE FIVE – BROWN EYES – BLONDE HAIR

Pat Skunk

Has illusions of grandeur. Insists on being called Patrick despite actually being christened 'Pat', which he considers a name as common as cow pat on a farm.

AGE SIX – GREEN EYES – BROWN HAIR

CATEGORY 2: SMELLINESS SCORE

1/10

This score denotes a poo with almost no smell. A desirable score for most people, but one that would cause the Skunk family to consider disowning you.

7/10

A seriously stinky poo, think foetid sewer water with overtones of fatberg scrapings.

9/10

Nearly the stinkiest of all turds, a poo this smelly will cause you to beg for a gas mask. Some things in life once seen cannot be unseen. This smell cannot be unsmelt.

CATEGORY 3: FAVOURITE NURSERY RHYME

Humpty Dump-ty

One family member gets almost philosophical as they discuss whether the dump in this story is 'great' as in wonderful, or merely very large. They like to think it could be both.

Sleeping Pooty

Following the trend for realism in fiction, this nursery rhyme makes you graphically aware of the fact you can fart in your sleep.

The Guffin' Man

If you know the guffin' man and you see him coming, then you also know it's time to run away pronto.

Finally, a series of clues are included that provide everything you'll need to be able to solve the puzzle logically:

- The brown-eyed Skunk loves reading about The Guffin' Man.
- The youngest member of the family didn't do the smelliest poo, nor did they do the least smelly poo.
- John never gets philosophical when thinking about nursery rhymes.
- The child with blonde hair didn't do the smelliest poo.

The key fact that will enable you to reveal the guilty party is always listed in bold at the end of the clues, as follows:

- **The disappointing poo only registered as 1/10 on the SmellScale™.**

HOW TO SOLVE

Start by taking the first clue: **The brown-eyed Skunk loves reading about The Guffin' Man.**

To interpret this clue, Inspector Poupe must consult the suspect notes in his case file. Doing so tells him that Lou Skunk is the brown-eyed suspect. Therefore Lou Skunk's favourite nursery rhyme is that old classic, The Guffin' Man, which we can mark with a tick where 'Lou Skunk' meets 'The Guffin' Man' in the grid.

<table>
<tr><th></th><th>Humpty Dump-ty</th><th>Sleeping Pooty</th><th>The Guffin' Man</th><th>1/10</th><th>7/10</th><th>9/10</th></tr>
<tr><td>John Skunk</td><td></td><td></td><td></td><td></td><td></td><td></td></tr>
<tr><td>Lou Skunk</td><td></td><td></td><td>✓</td><td></td><td></td><td></td></tr>
<tr><td>Pat Skunk</td><td></td><td></td><td></td><td></td><td></td><td></td></tr>
<tr><td>1/10</td><td></td><td></td><td></td><td colspan="3"></td></tr>
<tr><td>7/10</td><td></td><td></td><td></td><td colspan="3"></td></tr>
<tr><td>9/10</td><td></td><td></td><td></td><td colspan="3"></td></tr>
</table>

After noting this down in his grid, the Inspector soon realises that if Lou Skunk's favourite nursery rhyme is The Guffin' Man, then it can't be Humpty Dump-ty or Sleeping Pooty. What's more, The Guffin' Man cannot be the favourite rhyme of John or Pat Skunk. Inspector Poupe crosses these off in the grid accordingly:

	Humpty Dump-ty	Sleeping Pooty	The Guffin' Man	1/10	7/10	9/10
John Skunk			✗			
Lou Skunk	✗	✗	✓			
Pat Skunk			✗			
1/10						
7/10						
9/10						

This brings Inspector Poupe to his second clue: **The youngest member of the family didn't do the smelliest poo, nor did they do the least smelly poo.**

Again, the inspector consults his case file. Doing so tells him that John Skunk is the youngest member of the Skunk family. As his poos are neither the smelliest nor the least smelly, he can eliminate the smelliness scores of 1/10 and 9/10 for little John:

	Humpty Dump-ty	Sleeping Pooty	The Guffin' Man	1/10	7/10	9/10
John Skunk			✗	✗		✗
Lou Skunk	✗	✗	✓			
Pat Skunk			✗			
1/10						
7/10						
9/10						

Doing so leaves him with just one possibility: John Skunk's poos score a mediocre 7/10 on the smelliness scale. Inspector Poupe notes this in his grid, eliminating the other suspects from that score accordingly.

	Humpty Dump-ty	Sleeping Pooty	The Guffin' Man	1/10	7/10	9/10
John Skunk			✗	✗	✓	✗
Lou Skunk	✗	✗	✓		✗	
Pat Skunk			✗		✗	
1/10						
7/10						
9/10						

The Inspector turns his attention to his third clue of the case: **John never gets philosophical when thinking about nursery rhymes.**

"Hmm...what could this mean?" he ponders. However, all is revealed when he consults the description of Humpty Dump-ty to find that "one family member is almost philosophical as they discuss whether the dump in this story is 'great' as in wonderful, or just very large". The clue must therefore be telling him that John's favourite rhyme is not Humpty Dump-ty, as John "is never philosophical when thinking about nursery rhymes". Inspector Poupe adds this deduction to his grid:

	Humpty Dump-ty	Sleeping Pooty	The Guffin' Man	1/10	7/10	9/10
John Skunk	✗		✗	✗	✓	✗
Lou Skunk	✗	✗	✓		✗	
Pat Skunk			✗		✗	
1/10						
7/10						
9/10						

In doing so, he sees that the only remaining person who could possibly have Humpty Dump-ty as their favourite nursery rhyme is Pat Skunk. Likewise, the only remaining nursery rhyme which could be John Skunk's favourite is Sleeping Pooty. The inspector grins as he notes down these findings:

	Humpty Dump-ty	Sleeping Pooty	The Guffin' Man	1/10	7/10	9/10
John Skunk	✗	✓	✗	✗	✓	✗
Lou Skunk	✗	✗	✓		✗	
Pat Skunk	✓	✗	✗		✗	
1/10						
7/10						
9/10						

The Inspector moves on to his fourth clue: **The child with blonde hair didn't do the smelliest poo.**

Referring again to his suspect notes, Inspector Poupe sees that Lou Skunk is the blonde-haired child. He can therefore deduce that Lou Skunk's poo did not score 9/10 on the SmellScale™:

	Humpty Dump-ty	Sleeping Pooty	The Guffin' Man	1/10	7/10	9/10
John Skunk	✗	✓	✗	✗	✓	✗
Lou Skunk	✗	✗	✓		✗	✗
Pat Skunk	✓	✗	✗		✗	
1/10						
7/10						
9/10						

Again, this leaves the Inspector only one possibility – Lou Skunk's poos score a pitiful 1/10, while Pat Skunk's turds must be a potent 9/10:

	Humpty Dump-ty	Sleeping Pooty	The Guffin' Man	1/10	7/10	9/10
John Skunk	✗	✓	✗	✗	✓	✗
Lou Skunk	✗	✗	✓	✓	✗	✗
Pat Skunk	✓	✗	✗	✗	✗	✓
1/10						
7/10						
9/10						

With these deductions in place, Inspector Poupe has enough information to fill in the remainder of the grid. All he has to do is transfer each suspect's poo score to the column for their respective nursery rhyme.

For example, John Skunk's favourite nursery rhyme is Sleeping Pooty and his poo scored 7/10, therefore Sleeping Pooty can be matched to the 7/10 rating.

	Humpty Dump-ty	Sleeping Pooty	The Guffin' Man	1/10	7/10	9/10
John Skunk	✗	✓	✗	✗	✓	✗
Lou Skunk	✗	✗	✓	✓	✗	✗
Pat Skunk	✓	✗	✗	✗	✗	✓
1/10		✗				
7/10	✗	✓	✗			
9/10		✗				

Poupe applies the same logic to Lou Skunk, whose poo scored a pathetic 1/10 and whose favourite nursery rhyme is The Guffin' Man. The Guffin' Man can therefore be matched to a score of 1/10. Finally, Humpty Dump-ty is the favourite of Pat Skunk whose poo scored the impressive 9/10. Humpty Dump-ty can therefore be matched to a score of 9/10.

	Humpty Dump-ty	Sleeping Poofy	The Guffin' Man	1/10	7/10	9/10
John Skunk	✗	✓	✗	✗	✓	✗
Lou Skunk	✗	✗	✓	✓	✗	✗
Pat Skunk	✓	✗	✗	✗	✗	✓
1/10	✗	✗	✓			
7/10	✗	✓	✗			
9/10	✓	✗	✗			

The final clue tells Inspector Poupe who his guilty suspect is.

In this case, his final clue is: **The disappointing poo only registered as 1/10 on the SmellScale™.**

The inspector therefore knows that the culprit he is looking for did a poo scoring 1/10. Consulting his grid, he collates all his information to answer the three big questions of the case:

> Who did the poo?
> What did it score on the SmellScale™?
> What is the pooer's favourite nursery rhyme?

His answers are as follows:

> Lou Skunk did the poo.
> Her poo scored 1/10 on the Smell Scale™.
> Her favourite nursery rhyme is The Guffin' Man.

And that's all there is to it! Inspector Poupe has cracked the case, restoring logic and order to a chaotic, poo-filled world.

The book is divided into three sections, containing 20 easy, 20 medium and 20 hard cases respectively. You may also find yourself needing to consult the exhibits in Inspector Poupe's possession, or unravelling tricky codes. But fear not! It's all in a day's work for this disgusting detective. If you get stuck at any point, you can consult the answers at the back of the book.

Whilst we recommend solving the puzzles while on the toilet, feel free to solve them wherever and whenever you like. You don't even have to tackle them in order. Now it's time to grab a peg for your nose, and start solving!

LOOSE STOOLS: EASY

EXHIBIT A

The contents of Inspector Poupe's detective kit

THE POOP SCOOP NEWSPAPER

Inspector Poupe buys a copy every day; he likes to stay up to date with the latest news flush. Today's headline reads: "SJWC In Bust Up with Minister".

THE SWORD WITH THE BROWN HILT

A legendary weapon once wielded by Sir Galahadashit of the Round Toilet. Poupe found it in a charity shop.

CIPHER RING

A cunning gadget for decoding ROT13, a cipher beloved by Professor Morifarty. Letters are shifted 13 places down the alphabet.

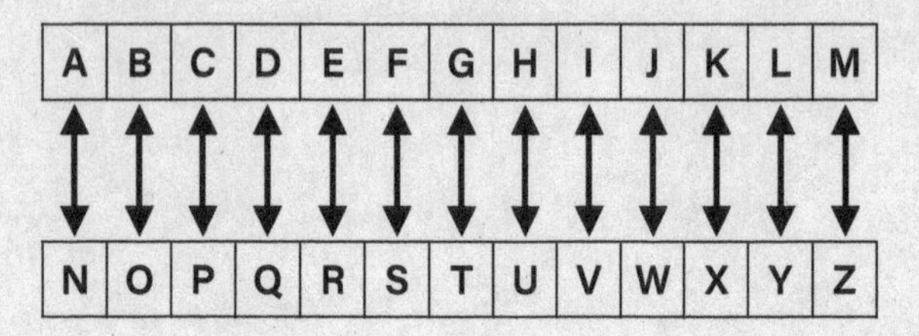

A	B	C	D	E	F	G	H	I	J	K	L	M
↕	↕	↕	↕	↕	↕	↕	↕	↕	↕	↕	↕	↕
N	O	P	Q	R	S	T	U	V	W	X	Y	Z

SIGNED SKULL

It once belonged to Laurence, a celebrated actor. No, it's not *his* skull. He just used to hold it when performing.

1. WHO DID THE POO?

A mysterious turd has appeared in an otherwise sparkling house share. As all three residents insist they aren't guilty, their landlord has no choice but to engage the professional services of Inspector Poupe.

SUSPECTS

Dr. Dung

This pro-proctologist has the guts to try any operation. They're not usually his guts.

5'8" – DARK BROWN EYES – BROWN HAIR

Lady Lav

An elegant woman with a dirty sense of humour. It's short for Lavinia, by the way.

5'6" – BLUE EYES – BLONDE HAIR

Mr. Manure

A retired farmer who delights in fertilising the fields with his 100% organic brand of homemade compost.

6'0" – LIGHT BROWN EYES – BALD HEAD

DINNER

Cheese	Fish	Sweetcorn
A wonderful slab of dairy goodness. Not for the lactose intolerant.	Stinks awfully on the plate. Stinks worse in the bowl.	Delicious, yellow and indigestible.

LOCATION

Garden	Kitchen	Living Room
The roses are always blooming. Just don't ask why...	Hygiene is of paramount importance to the landlord, so this is swabbed clean every weekend. After the latest incident, it's going to need a lot of swabbing.	Home to a plush carpet and communal plasma TV. No expense was spared.

CLUES

- The former farmer has grown enough sweetcorn for a lifetime. He refuses to eat it now.
- Dr. Dung was watching his favourite TV show in the living room – Holby Shitty.
- Lady Lav won't eat anything that once swam.
- Mr. Manure was making his dinner in the kitchen.
- The blue-eyed suspect despises sweetcorn.
- **The turd reeked of fish.**

	LOCATION			DINNER		
	Garden	Kitchen	Living Room	Cheese	Fish	Sweetcorn
SUSPECTS						
Dr. Dung						
Lady Lav						
Mr. Manure						
DINNER						
Cheese						
Fish						
Sweetcorn						

WHO DID THE POO?

WHAT DID THEY EAT?

WHERE WAS IT FOUND?

Suspects	Dinner	Location
Dr. Dung		
Lady Lav		
Mr. Manure		

2. GOURMET POOED

With three Michelin stars to its name, Le Grand Caca receives its fair share of entitled customers. After Lord Askwhiff makes a particularly snotty complaint about his main course, somebody decides to take revenge into their own hands. You could say Lord Askwhiff got his just 'desserts' when he ordered the chocolate pie. After taking one bite of the pie and realising what it contained, an outraged Askwhiff summons Inspector Poupe to deduce who decided to do a poo and mix it into the pie as a 'secret ingredient'.

SUSPECTS

Chef Derriere

Head chef at Le Grand Caca, Chef Derriere is feared by all of his kitchen staff. He is prone to fits of rage and cannot stand customer complaints. He is also notorious for his potty mouth, but is this reflected in his food?

6'0" – GREEN EYES – MOUSTACHE

Joe Bogs

The kitchen pot washer would have ample opportunity to slip something into the food. As far as he's concerned, it would serve Chef Derriere right to finally get a one-star review!

5'9" – BLUE EYES – CLEAN-SHAVEN

Suzie Stinkman

Waitress at Le Grand Caca, she often fails to hide her resentment towards customers and chefs alike. She dreams of becoming a famous poet and is sick of being shouted at and bossed around.

5'6" – BROWN EYES – FRECKLES

LUNCH

Cup of Coffee

A large dose of caffeine, perfect for the hustle and bustle of a restaurant. It certainly keeps bowel movements flowing.

Steak Frites

When in a gourmet restaurant, why not treat yourself to a gourmet lunch?

Tomato Soup

Homemade – not the stuff out of a can – finished off with a twist of black pepper.

REACTIONS

Blank Stare

One suspect kept a poker face the whole time. They were impossible to read.

Licking Lips

One suspect was clearly hungry. They licked their lips as the unsuspecting customer guzzled a 'chocolatey' dessert.

Smile

As the customer tucked into the pie, one suspect's face broke into an uncharacteristic smile.

CLUES

- As Lord Askwhiff ate the pie, a pair of green eyes stared blankly at the customer.
- The freckled face did not crack a smile.
- The waitress and the chef both hated tomatoes.
- Suzie Stinkman did not consume any caffeine.
- **The pie tasted strongly of coffee.**

		REACTIONS			LUNCH		
		Blank Stare	Licking Lips	Smile	Cup of Coffee	Steak Frites	Tomato Soup
SUSPECTS	Chef Derriere						
	Joe Bogs						
	Suzie Stinkman						
LUNCH	Cup of Coffee						
	Steak Frites						
	Tomato Soup						

WHO DID THE POO?

WHAT DID THEY HAVE FOR LUNCH?

WHAT WAS THEIR REACTION?

Suspects	Lunch	Reactions
Chef Derriere		
Joe Bogs		
Suzie Stinkman		

3. SMELT IT, DEALT IT

It's time for the debutante ball at the prestigious El Posho Hotel, the most nerve-racking event for any aspiring debutante. Three triplets have got there early to give themselves plenty of time to prepare for the ball. Indeed, they are the first to arrive, so sit down at the tables they'll be located at later on and munch on a snack to keep them going. Unfortunately, nerves have got the better of one of them, who has farted. Except not just any old fart – this is a proper stinker. Appalled, and worried she will have to cancel the event or pay for fumigation, the organiser calls in the services of Inspector Poupe. She has him on speed dial for occasions just like this; he arrives within minutes, the air still redolent with the foul odour. Whoever let that little beauty go, the organiser informs him, is not worthy of polite society and will be evicted from the ball post-haste.

Who does Poupe point the finger at?

SUSPECTS

Belle

The youngest of the three triplets by two minutes, and also the feistiest.

5'3" – RED HAIR – BLUE EYES

Danielle

The calmest of the three triplets, and also the eldest. Loves dressing up.

5'4" – BLONDE HAIR – BLUE EYES

Giselle

The loudest of the three and also the tallest, Giselle can be heard a mile away.

5'5" – BLONDE HAIR – BROWN EYES

LOCATION

Table 1	Table 2	Table 3
A square table that can accommodate five people and has a centrepiece of silver and gold balloons.	A rectangular table that sits eight people, and has confetti shaped like stars sprinkled in its centre.	A circular table that sits four and has a lovely centrepiece of scented red roses.

SNACK EATEN

Chocolate Bar	Crisps	Popcorn
Just a bar of solid milk chocolate in a golden wrapping, unexciting but does the job. The chocolate equal of a plain old glass of water.	Ready salted flavour in a red packet, the vanilla ice cream of crisps. A trusty favourite that hits the spot.	Salty popcorn in a small blue bag, sates hunger and that's about it. The margherita pizza of the popcorn world.

CLUES

- The crisps weren't eaten by anyone with blue eyes.
- Danielle's table seats the lowest number of people.
- Belle glared at her sibling munching a salty snack from a blue bag and told her to eat with her mouth closed.
- The person sitting at the starry table was not the tallest of the three siblings.
- **The farter consumed the snack in the blue packet.**

		SNACK EATEN			LOCATION		
		Chocolate Bar	Crisps	Popcorn	Table 1	Table 2	Table 3
SUSPECTS	Belle						
	Danielle						
	Giselle						
LOCATION	Table 1						
	Table 2						
	Table 3						

WHO DROPPED THE FART?

WHICH TABLE WERE THEY AT?

WHAT SNACK DID THEY EAT?

Suspects	Location	Snack Eaten
Belle		
Danielle		
Giselle		

4. A STUDY IN SCATLET

Inspector Poupe travels back in time to assist a detective even more famous than himself: Sherlock Holes, proverbially known as 'No Shit Sherlock'. Ostensibly, Poupe is helping him and Dr. Squatson track down Morifarty, 'the Napooleon of Crime', but the inspector tries to keep an open mind. He analyses their stool samples to find the receptacle they might have defecated in and their drug of choice.

SUSPECTS

Dr. Squatson

No Shit Sherlock's revolver-wielding sidekick and biographer. Every time he pulls the trigger, he lets one rip.

5'7" – DOCTOR – PLAYS THE RECORDER

No Shit Sherlock

A detective famous for pointing out the obvious.

6'1" – DETECTIVE – PLAYS THE VIOLIN

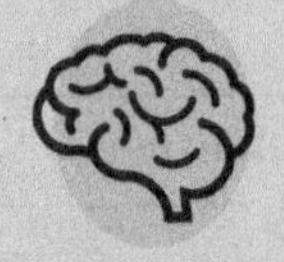

Professor Morifarty

No Shit Sherlock's flatulent nemesis. Despite his genius, he's never been able to figure out why people leave the room when he enters.

6'0" – PROFESSOR – PLAYS THE PIANO

RECEPTACLE

A Deerstalker Hat	A Policeman's Helmet	An Empty Perambulator
Holes's famous hat. It's a floppy brown thing.	You wouldn't, would you?	Prone to rolling down hills and being chased by concerned pedestrians.

DRUG

Cocaine	Opium	Tobacco
Taken as medicine by the Victorians, who were an odd bunch.	A very Victorian vice. A waxy green drug, it gives you waxy green stools.	You've heard of smoker's cough: now get ready for smoker's colon. Yes, it makes your shit stink as well.

CLUES

- Dr. Squatson has somehow acquired his friend's deerstalker hat.
- Morifarty refuses to touch tobacco, as it amplifies his flatulence.
- A confirmed bachelor, No Shit Sherlock has no need for a perambulator.
- Gur cvnavfg qbrf abg hfr pbpnvar, naq arvgure qbrf Qe. Fdhngfba. (Morifarty has encoded this clue. See Exhibit A for help.)
- **You are looking for an opium addict.**

	Cocaine	Opium	Tobacco	A Deerstalker Hat	A Policeman's Helmet	An Empty Perambulator
	DRUG			RECEPTACLE		
SUSPECTS: Dr. Squatson						
No Shit Sherlock						
Professor Morifarty						
RECEPTACLE: A Deerstalker Hat						
A Policeman's Helmet						
An Empty Perambulator						

WHO DID THE POO?

WHAT DID THEY POO IN?

WHAT ARE THEY ADDICTED TO?

Suspects	Receptacle	Drug
Dr. Squatson		
No Shit Sherlock		
Professor Morifarty		

5. VISITING THE CAMPSHITE

The 1st Crapstone Scouts are on their yearly jamboree. They arrive early and pitch their tents, but disaster looms: the toilets are on the other side of the campsite, and it's a cold, cold night. The next morning, their red-faced scoutmaster holds up a sticky object in a plastic bag. Until the culprit fesses up, nobody's going home. The scoutmaster enlists an old friend, Inspector Poupe, to help him identify the guilty child. He must figure out what everyone ate or drank the night before, and where they were located.

SUSPECTS

Ben Dover

What were his parents thinking? Seriously.

AGE 14 – BLACK HAIR – SCOUT

Cub Crud

Nobody wants to share a tent with Cub Crud. The poor lad reeks.

AGE 10 – BROWN HAIR – CUB

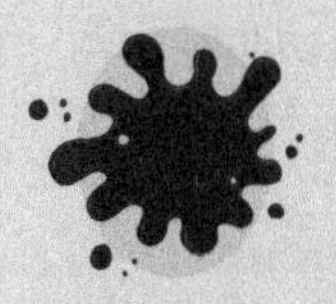

Sticky Stu

A reprehensible child who cannot be prevented from wiping his nose on his sleeve.

AGE 8 – BLOND HAIR – BEAVER

FOOD

Baked Beans	Hot Chocolate	Tuna Sandwich
Beans, beans, good for your heart. The more you eat, the more you fart!	A heaped spoonful of cocoa powder dissolved in boiling water. A delicious laxative.	This sandwich stewed in clingfilm for several days before it was eaten. The effects may be explosive.

LOCATION

By The Fence	By The Fire	Under The Trees
It's human nature to go to the toilet against fences and walls. Animals do the same, so watch your step.	The smouldering coals diffuse a pleasant warmth through the nearby air. They also help spread smells.	The leaves rustle, and owls can be heard shrieking in the treetops. Not a toilet for the faint-hearted.

CLUES

- Sticky Stu was seen wandering along the perimeter fence late last night, perhaps hoping to hop over it and run home.
- When Cub Crud warmed himself by the fire, his odour wafted through the camp.
- The youngest camper had their tuna sandwich stolen and eaten by one of the older boys so had to consume something else. It wasn't Cub Crud that stole and ate it – he's allergic to fish.
- The boy with blond hair sensibly didn't eat baked beans.
- **The bag of faeces was, quite literally, a beanbag.**

	LOCATION: By The Fence	LOCATION: By The Fire	LOCATION: Under The Trees	FOOD: Baked Beans	FOOD: Hot Chocolate	FOOD: Tuna Sandwich
SUSPECTS: Ben Dover						
SUSPECTS: Cub Crud						
SUSPECTS: Sticky Stu						
FOOD: Baked Beans						
FOOD: Hot Chocolate						
FOOD: Tuna Sandwich						

WHO DID THE POO?

WHAT HAD THEY EATEN OR DRUNK?

WHERE DID THEY DO IT?

Suspects	Food	Location
Ben Dover		
Cub Crud		
Sticky Stu		

6. POO IN THE ZOO

Inspector Poupe is asked to advise a nearby zoo on a feeding issue. He must figure out which animal is passing each type of stool so that the zookeepers can extend the diet of the animal with the preferred stool style to the rest of the large predators.

SUSPECTS

Bear

The zookeepers are bear-ly able to keep up with the mountains of dung this monster produces.

URSUS ARCTOS – MALE – AGE 14

Crocodile

Its turds float in the water. Unsurprisingly, none of the zookeepers want to dive in to retrieve them.

CROCODYLUS NILOTICUS – FEMALE – AGE 35

Lion

The king of the jungle. I'd be *lion* if I said its crap didn't smell.

PANTHERA LEO – MALE – AGE 10

CONSISTENCY

Flaky	Gloopy	Smooth
Dry, dusty and fragile stools. The animal passing these must be suffering from severe dehydration.	Wet, slushy and stinking to high heaven. This animal needs less water in its diet.	The golden mean of faeces. Sign of a happy, healthy animal.

DIET

Beef	Chicken	Salmon
Rich, red meat. It's expensive, but extremely nutritious.	The zookeepers don't bother to pluck the feathers. May tickle the throat.	Loved by bears, cats and crocodiles alike. Which of them is enjoying this delicacy?

CLUES

- Salmon are released into the crocodile's tank for her to hunt.
- The animal with the binomial name Ursus Arctos isn't fed chicken.
- The youngest animal doesn't have gloopy stools.
- The crocodile's dung is either flaky or smooth.
- The lion hasn't got flaky faeces.
- **The creature with the smooth turds is on the healthiest diet.**

		DIET			CONSISTENCY		
		Beef	Chicken	Salmon	Flaky	Gloopy	Smooth
SUSPECTS	Bear						
	Crocodile						
	Lion						
CONSISTENCY	Flaky						
	Gloopy						
	Smooth						

WHICH ANIMAL HAS THE HEALTHIEST DIET?

WHAT ARE ITS STOOLS LIKE?

WHAT IS IT EATING?

Suspects	Consistency	Diet
Bear		
Crocodile		
Lion		

7. WHODUNSHIT?

A blood-curdling scream rang out through Musturd Manor.
One guest had made a chilling discovery...

They had gone to pour themselves a glass of whisky when they glimpsed a dark shape in the corner of the room. Upon approaching, they saw the horrifying truth. They wanted to blame Dexter, the dog, but this stool was inhumanely human.

They immediately call Inspector Poupe and assemble the guests. After a long and ruthless interrogation, it is revealed that each of them had heeded nature's call at some point in the evening. Poupe must determine who did the offending poo, where it was found and what the offender 'cleaned up' with.

SUSPECTS

Colonel Musturd

A military man with impressive combat experience. The things he's seen would empty anyone's bowels.

6'1" – MOUSTACHE – AGE 56

Mrs. Wipe

An incredibly glamorous widow, often dressed in pristine white. Could be risky given the circumstances.

5'6" – PEARL NECKLACE – AGE 47

Professor Bum

An eminent scatologist on the cusp of publishing a seminal paper!

5'9" – MONOCLE – AGE 62

LOCATION

Billiard Room	Kitchen	Lounge
Perfect for entertaining the guests. Filled with green tables and stacks of board games.	The food looked delicious when it first appeared. Less so later.	Complete with velvet curtains and a roaring fire.

WIPED WITH

Newspaper	Scarf	Tissue
The user's excrement was well matched by the quality of the journalism.	Cut from the finest Himalayan cashmere. But needs must!	Perfectly adequate for the job.

CLUES

- Mrs. Wipe wiped the floor with her billiards opponent.
- The oldest suspect did not step foot in the kitchen.
- The youngest suspect only had a scarf and a newspaper to hand, so had to wipe with one of those.
- Professor Bum neglected to bring tissues, and he refused to spoil the Himalayan cashmere.
- **A soiled newspaper was found at the scene of the crime.**

	WIPED WITH			LOCATION		
	Newspaper	Scarf	Tissue	Billiard Room	Kitchen	Lounge
SUSPECTS						
Colonel Musturd						
Mrs. Wipe						
Professor Bum						
LOCATION						
Billiard Room						
Kitchen						
Lounge						

WHO DID THE POO?

WHERE?

WHAT DID THEY WIPE WITH?

Suspects	Location	Wiped With
Colonel Musturd		
Mrs. Wipe		
Professor Bum		

8. THREE IN A BED

Three friends, Ploppy, Skidder and Stinky, are saving money by sharing a hotel bed. Having indulged themselves in the hotel restaurant, the trio stumble upstairs and collapse onto the mattress. After a blissful night's sleep, the friends wake up to a nasty surprise; they now have a rather smelly fourth bedfellow. Who did the poo, what were they wearing and what had they eaten? It smells like another case for Inspector Poupe.

SUSPECTS

Ploppy

Known as a bit of a joker. Could this be another of their famous pranks?

5'8" – BROWN HAIR – TALKS IN SLEEP

Skidder

The quietest member of the group. Silent but deadly, perhaps?

6'2" – BLOND HAIR – SNORES

Stinky

Stinky by name, stinky by nature.

6'0" – GINGER HAIR – SLEEPWALKS

NIGHTWEAR

Dressing Gown	Pyjamas	Underwear
Made of wool and incredibly cosy.	Christmas-themed but too comfy not to wear all year round.	The boxers were only left on after lengthy negotiations.

DINNER

Mushroom Risotto	Roast Chicken	Spaghetti Bolognese
With mushrooms foraged by the chef himself. Let's hope he knows what he's doing.	The chef's speciality. The secret ingredient is talent.	Deliciously meaty, even the next day.

CLUES

- Skidder did not order spaghetti bolognese.
- Stinky found wool too warm to sleep in.
- Neither Skidder nor Ploppy ordered roast chicken.
- The snoring bedfellow slept in his underwear.
- **A pair of pyjama bottoms with brown stains were found hidden in the bathroom.**

		DINNER			NIGHTWEAR		
		Mushroom Risotto	Roast Chicken	Spaghetti Bolognese	Dressing Gown	Pyjamas	Underwear
SUSPECTS	Ploppy						
	Skidder						
	Stinky						
NIGHTWEAR	Dressing Gown						
	Pyjamas						
	Underwear						

WHO POOED IN THE BED?

WHAT WERE THEY WEARING?

WHAT DID THEY EAT FOR DINNER?

Suspects	Nightwear	Dinner
Ploppy		
Skidder		
Stinky		

9. TURDULENT PRIESTS

Inspector Poupe is called upon once more to investigate a case of the gravest import. Someone has defecated in the cathedral. Worse, the crime occurred when the cathedral was closed to the public, so the only suspects are three men of the cloth. A delicate case indeed, but Poupe handles it with his trademark panache.

SUSPECTS

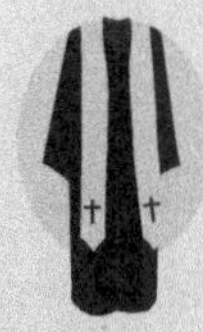

Canon Caca

His robes are long enough to wipe with and dark enough to not show the stains.

5'4" – BLOND HAIR – AGE 35

The Stinking Bishop

A slimy old prelate who's more fungus than man. The cheese is named for him.

6'1" – BALD – AGE 74

Vicar Viscous

So called because of the smoothness of his speech... and also the smoothness of his turds.

5'2" – BLACK HAIR – AGE 46

FOOD

Chocolate Teacakes	Communion Wafers	Jam Sandwich
Beloved by the clergy for their delightful marshmallowy interior.	Someone scoffed the whole box of wafers after forgetting their packed lunch.	Whoever ate this may find themselves in a sticky situation.

LOCATION

By The Altar	By The Font	In The Cloister
The sacred heart of the cathedral. Dumping a load here would be sacrilege.	Let's hope it is *by*, not in, or the next baby to be baptised is in trouble!	Where monks dwell away from the hustle and bustle of the world. Has their sanctuary been invaded?

CLUES

- The Stinking Bishop was at the altar. He considers the mere idea of eating communion wafers blasphemy.
- The monks insisted that they hadn't seen Canon Caca in the cloister.
- The wafers weren't eaten by the youngest man.
- The oldest priest didn't eat any teacakes.
- **The turd had a distinctive chocolate-marshmallowy odour.**

		By The Altar	By The Font	In The Cloister	Chocolate Teacakes	Communion Wafers	Jam Sandwich
		LOCATION			FOOD		
SUSPECTS	Canon Caca						
	Stinking Bishop						
	Vicar Viscous						
FOOD	Chocolate Teacakes						
	Communion Wafers						
	Jam Sandwich						

WHO DID THE POO?

WHAT HAD THEY EATEN?

WHERE WERE THEY?

Suspects	Food	Location
Canon Caca		
The Stinking Bishop		
Vicar Viscous		

10. KNIGHT SOIL

To hone his skills of deduction, Poupe is tackling a famous scandal from long ago that he has recently read about. It was 5:55pm on the 5th May, 555 AD, and King Arthur's royal nose wrinkled as he sat on his throne in Camelot, presiding over a grand feast. Someone had defecated during the fish course, and one of his knights was clearly the culprit. Poupe uses the facts of the case to link each knight to their emblem and outfit, in order to figure out who is to blame for the fact there is something fishy going on.

SUSPECTS

Sir Crapsalot

Once the greatest knight of the Round Toilet, and now an irritable, elderly man who struggles with incontinence. He can still quest when the opportunity arises.

AGE 67 – JOUSTS WON: 101 – BLUE EYES

Sir Galahadashit

Son of Sir Crapşalot. A pure and puissant knight who obtained the Holy Grail – and promptly used it as a toilet.

AGE 33 – JOUSTS WON: 73 – BROWN EYES

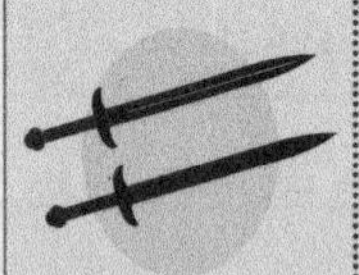

Sir Pooceval

One of King Arthur's 'privy knights', he never smells and tells.

AGE 42 – JOUSTS WON: 52 – GREEN EYES

EMBLEM

A Bogbrush Rampant

Stiff, spiky and stained. The knight who bears this on his shield is a prickly customer.

A Toilet Couchant

Borne by 'the Knight of the Can', this shield has been witness to a hundred flushes.

A Turd Issuant

Before you ask, it's brown paint. They're not *that* devoted to realism.

CLOTHING

Chain mail

You could try to squeeze one through the tiny holes, but I wouldn't recommend it.

Garderobe

Not your standard garderobe. This one is a long, loose garment which hides a chamber pot, so knights don't have to leave the table at feasts. Patent pending.

Plate armour

Awfully inconvenient when nature calls. However, the helmet is a convenient receptacle.

CLUES

- Sir Pooceval showed up to the feast in shining plate armour. Shining on the outside, at least.
- The oldest knight does not have a toilet couchant painted on his shield.
- The knight who once wielded the Sword with the Brown Hilt is not wearing a garderobe. (See Exhibit A.)
- The knight who's won 73 jousts bears neither the toilet couchant nor the turd issuant.
- **The culprit's emblem is the toilet couchant.**

	Chain mail	Garderobe	Plate armour	A Bogbrush Rampant	A Toilet Couchant	A Turd Issuant
	CLOTHING			EMBLEM		
SUSPECTS: Sir Crapsalot						
Sir Galahadashit						
Sir Pooceval						
EMBLEM: A Bogbrush Rampant						
A Toilet Couchant						
A Turd Issuant						

WHO DID THE POO?

WHAT WAS THEIR EMBLEM?

WHAT WERE THEY WEARING?

Suspects	Emblem	Clothing
Sir Crapsalot		
Sir Galahadashit		
Sir Pooceval		

11. JAIL TURDS

When the wardens of HM Prison Wormwood Wipes make their rounds in the morning, they're greeted by a noxious whiff. One of the prisoners has smashed the toilet in their cell and done their business on the cold stone floor. Inspector Poupe is asked to handle this delicate matter. (He wears gloves.) He connects each inmate to their most recent meal and the reason they're in the slammer, in order to work out who is to blame.

SUSPECTS

Dirty Dan

A dangerous desperado with low standards of personal hygiene and the strength to bend an iron bar.

6'3" – BLACK HAIR – PRISONER NUMBER 051

Foul Flo

Foetid, feculent and all-round filthy. Being in the cell next to her is considered a cruel and unusual punishment.

5'4" – SANDY-BROWN HAIR – PRISONER NUMBER 083

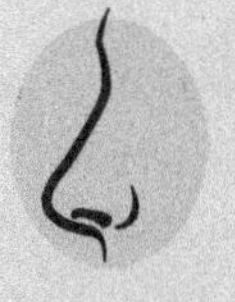

Pongy Pete

The pong is strong. It lingers long.

5'6" – GINGER HAIR – PRISONER NUMBER 029

FOOD

Bread and Water

The water has brown particles floating in it. The bread looks like dried mud. Bon appétit!

Mystery Meat

Blended, oversalted and tasteless meat. If it's not beef, then it's pork. If it's not pork, it's chicken. If it's not chicken... best not go there.

Porridge

Your stereotypical prison meal. Tedium given substance.

CRIME

Drink Driving

At the speed they were driving, it's a miracle the only damage was to their car.

Hooliganism

Travelling to foreign countries not to watch football but to fight foreign fans. Everyone needs a hobby.

Public Urination

Rather than pay 50p for a public lav, they went behind the bushes. Unfortunately, a police officer was lurking nearby, having just zipped up themselves.

CLUES

- Prisoner number 083 lost their driving licence after crashing through a hedge at 90mph. Breathalyser evidence showed they were three times over the legal limit.
- Foul Flo won't touch the canteen meat, as it "gives her wind something terrible".
- The ginger-haired convict is a notorious football hooligan.
- One of the inmates recently bent the iron bars in their window in an attempt to escape. As punishment, they've been banned from eating meat or porridge.
- **The stool was grey and slimy, just like prison porridge. That's clearly not a coincidence.**

		CRIME			FOOD		
		Drink Driving	Hooliganism	Public Urination	Bread and Water	Mystery Meat	Porridge
SUSPECTS	Dirty Dan						
	Foul Flo						
	Pongy Pete						
FOOD	Bread and Water						
	Mystery Meat						
	Porridge						

WHO DID THE POO?

WHAT HAD THEY EATEN?

WHAT WAS THEIR CRIME?

Suspects	Food	Crime
Dirty Dan		
Foul Flo		
Pongy Pete		

12. IT'S MURDER OUT THERE!

Lord 'Chewlip' Leopold got his nickname as he is always fretting about something, leading to the most unfortunate facial expression. Recently he's been overly vexed by a murder of crows pooing all over his beloved garden. Matters have come to a head since his neighbour, and rival, started feeding them leftover food which has increased the frequency of the droppings and turned Lord Chewlip's skin a strange puce colour.

One bird has now taken it too far and pooed on an object Lord Chewlip considers sacrosanct. Inspector Poupe has been called in to find out who did it. If successful, Lord Chewlip will give Poupe a £1,000 reward – now that's something to crow about.

SUSPECTS

Dash

A nippy blighter, the Bugatti Super Sport of crows, he flies away before Lord Chewlip can even open the door to shout at him.

91 CM WINGSPAN – 5 CM BEAK – CRIES "CA-CA"

Flappy

Flappy flies in a very singular manner, hence the name. But it works for him – he always gets away before Lord Chewlip can give him a piece of his mind.

100 CM WINGSPAN – 6 CM BEAK – CRIES "POO-POO"

Squawky

His loud call is every bit as annoying to Lord Chewlip as the droppings all over his precious garden.

93 CM WINGSPAN – 4 CM BEAK – CRIES "DOO-DOO"

LOCATION

Koi Pond

One expensive pond, filled with chunky koi carp that any passing heron would love to eat for breakfast, lunch or dinner. Adorned with the finest pond plants.

Sundial

The sundial is an object Lord Chewlip is very attached to. It has been in the family for generations, originally commissioned by his great-grandmother, God rest her soul.

Tropical Greenhouse

Lovely and warm inside with moist air, the perfect growing environment for some of the exotic plants that bring a rare smile to Lord Chewlip's face.

POO AROMA

Burnt Toast

A deeply unpleasant smell combining the aroma of smoke from the toaster with overtones of poo.

Dog Food

No prizes for guessing what the blighters must have eaten for their poo to smell of this. That neighbour has a lot to answer for.

Offal

All levels of wrong: consuming offal leads to poo that does indeed smell 'offal'. If evil had a smell, this would be it.

CLUES

- The bird whose cry sounds strangely like "ca-ca" never eats offal. He has standards.
- Squawky has been observed doing his business on the roof of the tropical greenhouse.
- Neither the bird with the largest wingspan nor the bird with the shortest wingspan have poo that smells like toast.
- The quickest bird loves to drop his little missiles into the pond: he likes the satisfying splash they make.
- **The object Lord Chewlip considers sacrosanct is a family heirloom.**

	Burnt Toast	Dog Food	Offal	Koi Pond	Sundial	Tropical Greenhouse
	POO AROMA			LOCATION		
SUSPECTS: Dash						
Flappy						
Squawky						
LOCATION: Koi Pond						
Sundial						
Tropical Greenhouse						

WHO DID THE POO?

WHERE DID THEY DO IT?

WHAT DID IT SMELL OF?

Suspects	Location	Poo Aroma
Dash		
Flappy		
Squawky		

13. TURD WHEEL

Terry, Robin and Cameron were an inseparable trio until two of them entered a relationship. They were eating ice cream together when they told the third, who immediately started crying and soiled themselves. Inspector Poupe, who happens to also be enjoying an ice cream nearby through sheer chance, quickly identifies and consoles the miserable 'turd wheel'.

SUSPECTS

Cameron

Energetic and expressive, Cameron is the trio's natural leader.

5'9" – BLACK HAIR – BLUE EYES

Robin

The trio's moral compass, Robin loves once and forever.

5'6" – BROWN HAIR – BROWN EYES

Terry

Indolent and intelligent, Terry is mostly happy to go with the flow.

5'7" – GINGER HAIR – GREEN EYES

ICE CREAM FLAVOUR

Chocolate	Strawberry	Vanilla
Don't let this drip on your trousers, or people might get the wrong idea.	The cheap stuff, so there's no real fruit. Artificial sweeteners loosen the bowels.	The basic flavour, sure, but it's still delicious.

OCCUPATION

Accountant	Dentist	Preschool Teacher
They crunch numbers all day, but did they remember to chew their food?	They probably wipe with toothpaste.	You would think that someone who toilet-trains children would be trained themselves, but that's not always the case.

CLUES

- The tallest of the three is a dentist.
- Terry isn't a fan of strawberry ice cream. Robin doesn't like strawberry or the most basic flavour.
- Terry crunches numbers for a living.
- **The turd stank of vanilla essence.**

		OCCUPATION			FLAVOUR		
		Accountant	Dentist	Preschool Teacher	Chocolate	Strawberry	Vanilla
SUSPECTS	Cameron						
	Robin						
	Terry						
FLAVOUR	Chocolate						
	Strawberry						
	Vanilla						

WHO DID THE POO?

WHAT WERE THEY EATING?

WHAT WAS THEIR OCCUPATION?

Suspects	Ice Cream Flavour	Occupation
Cameron		
Robin		
Terry		

14. THE BURDEN OF POOS

Court is now in session. The defendant takes to the stand. Their case rests on a crucial piece of evidence. Unfortunately, both the evidence and their reputation have been smeared. Somebody has used the item to clean up their own crimes. Poupe is summoned to deduce who has tampered with the evidence and where it happened.

SUSPECTS

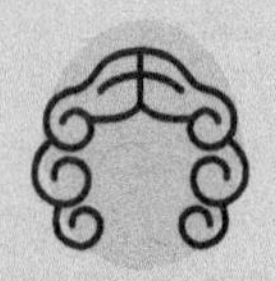

Barrister Bothamley

Decided to work in law purely because of how great they look in a wig.

5'7" – AUSTERE – BRACELET

Hugh Janus Esquire

A talented lawyer who, for some reason, never gets taken seriously.

6'3" – FRIENDLY – WEDDING RING

Judge Doodie

She's firm but she's fair, much like her stools.

5'8" – WISE – WATCH

LOCATION

Bin	Garden	Toilet
The toilet was occupied. This was the second best thing.	Filled with blooming rosebushes. Their fragrant aroma disguises any unpleasant smells.	Hasn't been cleaned for months, but still the most dignified option.

WIPED WITH

Banknote	Legal Documents	Socks
The legal profession certainly pays well!	A stack of incredibly tedious paperwork.	A surprisingly effective tool, although the amount of friction is not too pleasant.

CLUES

- Judge Doodie did her business in a toilet, but was caught out by the lack of toilet paper.
- With the toilet occupied, the friendly lawyer was forced to squat behind a rosebush.
- The wisest of the suspects is far too professional to wipe themselves on legal documents.
- Neither Judge Doodie nor Hugh Janus Esquire wiped themselves with an item of clothing.
- **When the culprit was finished with them, the legal documents were entirely unusable.**

	WIPED WITH			LOCATION		
	Banknote	Legal Documents	Socks	Bin	Garden	Toilet
SUSPECTS: Barrister Bothamley						
Hugh Janus Esquire						
Judge Doodie						
LOCATION: Bin						
Garden						
Toilet						

WHO SOILED THE EVIDENCE?

WHERE DID THEY POO?

WHAT DID THEY WIPE WITH?

Suspects	Location	Wiped With
Barrister Bothamley		
Hugh Janus Esquire		
Judge Doodie		

15. THE CASE OF THE BLOCKED LATRINE

Julie got home from a long day of lectures desperate for a bit of 'me time'. However, when she went to relieve herself, she found the toilet bowl overflowing! Which of her student housemates was responsible for this monstrous scene? Julie immediately calls Inspector Poupe. By finding out which toilet each housemate used and what they had for dinner, the inspector will soon sniff out the culprit!

SUSPECTS

Sasha Shartman

She's done a few jobbies in her time. Could this be her biggest to date?

5'2" – SCOTTISH – ONE POO A DAY

Sergio Poorez

Studying abroad can be hard. The toilet is an oasis of calm for young Sergio.

6'3" – SPANISH – THREE POOS A DAY

Turdie Brown

The others find her extremely uptight. It's hard to believe she even goes to the toilet.

5'4" – ENGLISH – TWO POOS A DAY

TOILET

Downstairs

The high water levels result in some unpleasant splash-back, but the window has a nice view of the garden.

Loft

Seat is low down to encourage a healthy squatting position.

Upstairs

Has a very weak flush. Bowel movements here are for risk-seekers only.

DINNER

Beetroot Soup

Bright pink, nutritious and delicious.

Chickpea Stew

A healthy dose of fibre to get things moving.

Spinach Pie

A snot-green dish worthy of Poopeye himself.

CLUES

- The Scottish housemate had beetroot soup for dinner.
- Sergio Poorez did not eat the green dish at dinner.
- Sasha Shartman did not poo upstairs or in the loft.
- Turdie Brown does not mind splash-back or a low seat.
- **When Julie got home, there were bits of chickpea in the overflowing bowl.**

		DINNER			TOILET	
	Beetroot Soup	Chickpea Stew	Spinach Pie	Downstairs	Loft	Upstairs
SUSPECTS Sasha Shartman						
Sergio Poorez						
Turdie Brown						
TOILET Downstairs						
Loft						
Upstairs						

WHO BLOCKED THE TOILET?

WHICH TOILET WAS BLOCKED?

TRACES OF WHAT FOOD WERE FOUND IN THE BOWL?

Suspects	Toilet	Dinner
Sasha Shartman		
Sergio Poorez		
Turdie Brown		

16. DIRTY PROTEST

Protesters have stormed the nation's capital to fight for a better world. While some might be happy to sit back and watch the world burn, some people really do give a shit... as one unfortunate bystander found out. Poupe is called in to deduce who threw the poo, where they launched their missile and in the name of what cause.

SUSPECTS

Freedump Fighter

Spends most of their life in online spats, but isn't afraid to get their hands dirty in the real world.

6'7" – CHEWS GUM – AGE 23

Poshitical Activist

Spilt their guts during an impassioned speech, and maybe afterwards as well.

5'8" – VAPES – AGE 32

SJWC

They will do anything to defend their cause, anything at all.

5'3" – SMOKES CIGARS – AGE 57

LOCATION

Government Building	International Bank	Town Square
Arty farty had a political party.	The perfect place to leave a deposit.	A scenic location for an alfresco poo.

POLITICAL CAUSE

Legalise Time Travel	Tax Imaginary Friends	Votes for Dogs
If only we could go back and legalise it sooner.	For too long these people have slipped through the cracks. They must give something back!	It's time man's best friend became man's best constituent.

CLUES

- The Freedump Fighter does not want to legalise time travel or give dogs the vote.
- One protester was seen arguing with a government official in their place of work. They even made the papers. (See Exhibit A.)
- The poshitical activist did not visit the bank.
- The impassioned speech given was not about canine voting rights.
- **A turd was launched in the name of taxation.**

		Political Cause			Location		
		Legalise Time Travel	Tax Imaginary Friends	Votes for Dogs	Government Building	International Bank	Town Square
Suspects	Freedump Fighter						
	Poshitical Activist						
	SJWC						
Location	Government Building						
	International Bank						
	Town Square						

WHO THREW THE POO?

WHERE WERE THEY?

WHAT WERE THEY CAMPAIGNING FOR?

Suspects	Location	Political Cause
Freedump Fighter		
Poshitical Activist		
SJWC		

17. MESS IN THE MESS

Inspector Poupe receives a summons to the local military base. Somebody has made a mess... in the officers' mess. After matching each officer to what they last ate and drank, Poupe quickly identifies the culprit.

SUSPECTS

Brigadier Bowel

As a brigadier, Bowel outranks both Colon and Midden. She claims not to know anything about the mess, but is she trying to put the blame on her subordinates?

5'8" – LONG HAIR – FRIENDLY

Colonel Colon

A stout man who grumbles a lot (through his mouth and his stomach).

5'7" – BALD – IRRITABLE

Major Midden

After twenty years of hard campaigning, this grizzled veteran no longer cares about hygiene. His turds are tough as old leather.

6'0" – SIDEBURNS – ALOOF

LAST ATE

French Onion Soup	Ham and Egg	Sushi
A delicious dish of caramelised onions topped with melted cheese. They have it lush, those officers.	Simple canteen food: a hunk of gammon with a greasy egg on top.	Slices of raw salmon, tuna and shrimp wrapped in rice and seaweed.

LAST DRANK

Orange Juice	Red Wine	Tea
Freshly squeezed citrus, with pips.	Made with real British grapes.	The discerning person's beverage of choice. Leaves brown stains.

CLUES

- The most senior officer on trial had onion breath.
- Colonel Colon is allergic to citrus. In an almost impossible coincidence, so is Brigadier Bowel.
- The bald gentleman had sushi for lunch.
- "Tea?" the most irritable officer grumbled. "I don't – like – tea!" Dashing their cup on the floor, they ordered a different type of drink.
- **The mess in the mess stank of booze.**

	LAST DRANK			LAST ATE		
	Orange Juice	Red Wine	Tea	French Onion Soup	Ham and Egg	Sushi
SUSPECTS: Brigadier Bowel						
Colonel Colon						
Major Midden						
LAST ATE: French Onion Soup						
Ham and Egg						
Sushi						

WHO DID THE POO?

WHAT HAD THEY EATEN?

WHAT HAD THEY DRUNK?

Suspects	Last Ate	Last Drank
Brigadier Bowel		
Colonel Colon		
Major Midden		

18. POONAIL AND I

Poonail is a serious and potentially fatal condition. It may be contracted during the wiping process when a finger comes into contact with faecal matter, trapping the poo beneath the nail. When traces of brown matter appear on a household object, Inspector Poupe suspects one resident is concealing a severe case of poonail. Find out who touched what, suss out their wiping techniques and track down the contaminated housemate.

SUSPECTS

Bob Logs

A serious high-flying businessman who is far too busy to wash his hands.

5'7" – SUIT AND TIE – QUIFF

Di Rea

A passionate eco-warrior who uses as little paper as possible. Could her fingers be brown as well as green?

5'8" – LONG, FLOWING SKIRT – CURLY HAIR

Winnie Pooh

A thoroughly lovely woman but with a slightly odd smell. Nobody can bring themselves to tell her.

5'4" – PINK DRESS – PONYTAIL

LAST TOUCHED

Door Handle	Light Switch	TV Remote Control
One of the filthiest objects known to man.	Brown stains don't show up in the dark.	The most sought-after object in the house.

WIPING TECHNIQUE

Flat	Fold	Scrunch
Maximises surface area but can be susceptible to breakage.	Bolstering the paper with folds should prevent any breakage, hopefully preventing a case of poonail.	A great technique for getting in the cracks.

CLUES

- The businessman does not have time to scrunch or fold his toilet paper.
- The eco-warrior did not touch the door handle.
- Di Rea is happy to scrunch or keep it flat: she likes mixing things up a bit.
- Winnie Pooh watched TV straight after going to the toilet.
- **Traces of poo were found on the door handle.**

		TECHNIQUE			LAST TOUCHED		
		Flat	Fold	Scrunch	Door Handle	Light Switch	TV Remote Control
SUSPECTS	Bob Logs						
	Di Rea						
	Winnie Pooh						
LAST TOUCHED	Door Handle						
	Light Switch						
	TV Remote Control						

WHO HAD THE POONAIL?

WHAT DID THEY TOUCH?

WHAT WAS THEIR WIPING TECHNIQUE?

Suspects	Last Touched	Wiping Technique
Bob Logs		
Di Rea		
Winnie Pooh		

19. POO IN THE POOL

It's a family day out at Crapton Baths. All is going swimmingly until a mysterious shape is spotted lurking in the water. Thanks to the unwelcome turd, the pool must be evacuated. Who is behind the floating faeces? Poupe is called in to deduce where the suspects were when the offending item was unleashed and why they might commit such a crime.

SUSPECTS

Baby Loo Loo

She may be adorable, but don't let that fool you.

BLUE EYES – PINK SWIMSUIT – ARMBANDS

Daddy Doo Doo

Always wears brown trunks to the pool. Suspicious?

GREEN EYES – BROWN TRUNKS – SWIMMING CAP

Grandma Gastro

She may be fit and active but old age has taken its toll on her bowels.

HAZEL EYES – BLUE SWIMSUIT – GOGGLES

LOCATION

Changing Rooms	Pool	Showers
Where the screaming kids run riot.	Thankfully treated with a large dose of chlorine.	Either scalding hot or freezing cold – there's no in between.

MOTIVE

Accident	Fun	Hates Swimming
Swimming can be so relaxing... perhaps too relaxing?	Sometimes there's no other reason.	The perfect excuse to evacuate the pool.

CLUES

- Grandma Gastro and Daddy Doo Doo would never do a poo for such a trivial reason as mere fun – there'd have to be some other reason for it.
- The person wearing goggles adores swimming.
- Baby Loo Loo was taken to the showers for a wash.
- Daddy Doo Doo stayed away from the screaming kids.
- **The poo was found floating in the deep end.**

	MOTIVE: Accident	MOTIVE: Fun	MOTIVE: Hates Swimming	LOCATION: Changing Rooms	LOCATION: Pool	LOCATION: Showers
SUSPECTS: Baby Loo Loo						
SUSPECTS: Daddy Doo Doo						
SUSPECTS: Grandma Gastro						
LOCATION: Changing Rooms						
LOCATION: Pool						
LOCATION: Showers						

WHO DID THE POO?

WHERE DID THEY DO IT?

WHAT WAS THEIR MOTIVE?

Suspects	Location	Motive
Baby Loo Loo		
Daddy Doo Doo		
Grandma Gastro		

20. THE SHITSHOW MUST GO ON

Inspector Poupe attends a performance of *Hamlet* in which tragedy becomes farce. The audience is briefly evacuated after a foul smell spreads across the room. Even on his night off Poupe finds himself called into action, here having to work out which actor did the poo, who they were playing, and where they were standing.

SUSPECTS

Ian

A splendid actor with a booming voice and booming bowels.

5'7" – GREY HAIR – AGE 62

Laurence

A doyen of the stage, Laurence has played the leading role in every one of Shakespeare's plays, from *King Rear* to the *Taming of the Loo.*

6'2" – WHITE HAIR – AGE 70

Mark

A markedly successful actor, this crap-tastrophe could destroy his career.

5'9" – BROWN HAIR – AGE 53

PART

Hamlet	King Claudius	Polonius
"To be or not to be, that is the question." A better question might be: was it him?	The usurper King of Denmark, he wears voluminous robes that could easily conceal a crap.	A bumbling old man stabbed by Hamlet in Act 3. Perhaps the sword punctured his bowels.

LOCATION

Centre Stage	In The Wings	Stage Right
The focus of attention. If you soil yourself here, there's no escaping scrutiny.	Where actors wait to enter the stage – and sometimes shit themselves from sheer terror.	Just to the right of the main performer. You could attempt a surreptitious crap here, but don't expect to get away with it.

CLUES

- For once, the white-haired actor missed out on the title role.
- Ian, playing Polonius, was not in the wings or stage right when someone lost a battle with their bowels.
- The actor who once gave Poupe a signed skull (see Exhibit A) was either centre stage or stage right at the moment of truth.
- **The actor playing King Claudius shamed himself with a sudden shit-fart combo, known colloquially as a 'shart'.**

	LOCATION			PART		
	Centre Stage	In The Wings	Stage Right	Hamlet	King Claudius	Polonius
SUSPECTS Ian						
Laurence						
Mark						
PART Hamlet						
King Claudius						
Polonius						

WHO DID THE POO?

WHO WERE THEY PLAYING?

WHERE WERE THEY STANDING?

Suspects	Part	Location
Ian		
Laurence		
Mark		

SLIGHT STRAINING: MEDIUM

EXHIBIT B

The kit Inspector Poupe brings to tackle trickier cases

A ROMAN POOPARIUS

This sweet-smelling coin was given to Inspector Poupe by an archaeologist friend of his.

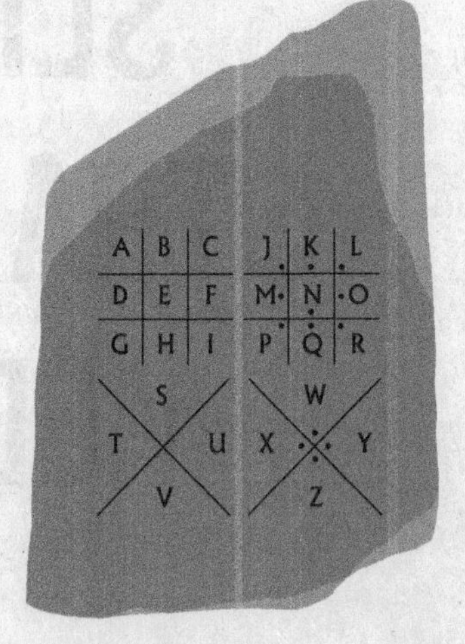

PIGPOO STONE

This artefact supposedly contains the key to deciphering the language of ancient aliens. Inspector Poupe can't remember how it came into his possession.

BROWN-TINTED GLASSES

These belonged to the supervillain Loocifer until they were punched off his face by one of the heroes. Poupe picked them up.

9-IRON CLUB

An expert in all things hole-related, Inspector Poupe is an avid golf fan. He recently acquired an old club of Will Whiffgift's, his favourite golfer of all time.

1. WHO GOT THE RUNS?

Waterloo Cricket Club have been playing a grudge match against local rivals. Unfortunately whilst some players have been in the runs today, one player has had the runs in a rather more literal sense. The incident happened in the changing room post match, and the embarrassed player quickly shoved his not-so-white whites into the wash basket along with those of three of his teammates.

The team coach is none too amused, quickly realising it's not mud but poo stains on the trousers he has just picked up. After washing his hands, outraged by the disrespect, he calls Inspector Poupe to get to the bottom of it, literally. After matching first names to surnames and players to their snacks and scores, which of the four does Poupe call out on review?

SUSPECTS

Drew

Drew is best friends with Jack, his fellow bowler. The team joker, he loves making his pals crease up.

6'1" – CREW CUT – GREEN EYES

Jack

Jack is very talented with ball in hand. The team's star bowler, his raw pace will hit you for six.

6'2" – SHAVED HEAD – BROWN EYES

John

Captain of the team, he is arrogant and potty-mouthed. Good with a bat, though.

5'6" – SPIKY HAIR – BROWN EYES

Louie

The wicketkeeper, he spends a lot of time on his knees.

5'10" – MULLET – BLUE EYES

SURNAME

Dunny

An unfortunate surname, but there are worse in the team. The family hail from Dunedin, New Zealand, so maybe Dunny is an unfortunate contraction of that city's name.

Longbottom

The origin of this surname is uncertain, but it's a bum deal if you're saddled with it.

McWhiffy

The McWhiffy clan apparently have a loo brush on their family shield, though this rumour probably started in the changing room, like so many.

Smellie

Master Smellie always wears lashings of aftershave, determined as he is to avoid nominative determinism.

RUNS SCORED

0

This score is known as a duck, and when someone is out for a duck they usually shout loudly a word that rhymes with it...

13

Unlucky for some. Specifically unlucky for the player who got out for this poor score today.

87

Known as 'the devil's number' it is considered unlucky by Aussies, though being British the person who scored this was jolly happy.

111

This score is known as a Nelson, since he is alleged to have had one eye, one arm and one leg towards the end of his life.

TEATIME SNACK

Beans On Toast

A wise choice for someone who wants their running between the wickets to be sped up by the power of the farts constantly being expelled from their derriere.

Sausage Roll

A meaty snack, and an apposite choice for the player who chose it as they drive a banger.

Scotch Egg

Chunky and meaty, this eggy snack is sure to cause smelly farts that will knock opposition bowlers off their game.

Tuna Sandwich

Topped with a layer of mustard, or should that be 'must turd', this hot, fishy snack could certainly lead to something of a sticky wicket.

CLUES

- The person who ate a food sure to speed them up between the wickets never benefitted from that fact as they scored a duck.
- Master McWhiffy scoffed a Scotch egg. His teammate Jack Smellie had a different snack.
- John's family do not hail from New Zealand. His score would be considered unlucky by an Australian.
- McWhiffy was the only player to score a century – it's his first ever three-figure score.
- The second-tallest of the four players watched two teammates eat a Scotch egg and beans on toast whilst munching on his own snack of choice.
- The person whose surname is a 'bum deal' hates fish.
- **The mystery pooper wasn't having a good day – they scored a duck.**

		TEATIME SNACK				RUNS SCORED				SURNAME			
		Beans On Toast	Sausage Roll	Scotch Egg	Tuna Sandwich	0	13	87	111	Dunny	Longbottom	McWhiffy	Smellie
SUSPECTS	Drew												
	Jack												
	John												
	Louie												
SURNAME	Dunny												
	Longbottom												
	McWhiffy												
	Smellie												
RUNS SCORED	0												
	13												
	87												
	111												

WHAT IS THEIR SURNAME?

HOW MANY RUNS DID THEY SCORE?

WHO HAD THE RUNS?

WHAT SNACK DID THEY CONSUME?

Suspects	Surname	Runs Scored	Teatime Snack
Drew			
Jack			
John			
Louie			

2. UP THE GUFF

It's rush hour on Tuesday evening and the bus is heaving. There are just three places left, yet there appear to be four pregnant women in need of a seat. A conundrum indeed! However, Inspector Poupe soon realises that only three of these women are genuinely pregnant – one simply has a bad case of trapped wind. Which of these bumps is purely the product of an upset stomach? Poupe must identify the faker, her relationship status, the food that irritates her bowels and the last thing she ate.

SUSPECTS

Emma Bidet

A high-powered career woman who loves her work. She's happy to have kids, as long as she can be the dad.

5'8" – BLUE EYES – AMBITIOUS

Kate Colon

Most of her dumps already feel like going into labour.

5'7" – BROWN EYES – SARCASTIC

Lisa Bogroll

Has potty-trained enough men to be well-qualified for motherhood.

5'9" – GREEN EYES – ENIGMATIC

Megan McTurdy

Has recently discovered adult nappies and hasn't looked back since.

5'6" – GREY EYES – POLITE

RELATIONSHIP STATUS

Complicated

So complicated they could make a TV show about it. Maybe one day they will.

Divorced

A million pounds of alimony can't heal a broken heart... can it?

Married

Her husband Terry spends most of his time on the bog. A man's toilet is his castle.

Single

Refuses to deal with another person's shit, either literal or metaphorical.

FOOD INTOLERANCE

Dairy

Some guy threw a block of cheese at my head. I said, how...

Onion

The most profound vegetable. So many layers.

Tomato

Fruit or vegetable, it's a formidable nemesis.

Wheat

So delicious it may be worth the pain.

LAST MEAL

Cheeseburger	Margherita Pizza
Oozing with mayo and impossible to eat without making a mess.	With a mozzarella cheese pull that goes on for miles.
Penne Arrabiata	**Salade Niçoise**
Undeniably the worst pasta shape, but a delicious sauce nonetheless.	The anchovy dressing is sure to keep the suitors at bay.

CLUES

- The singleton detests mayo.
- The person with the wheat intolerance ate the arrabiata, unable to resist its allure.
- The tallest suspect is, perhaps unusually, intolerant to tomatoes.
- The divorcee happily spent her ex-husband's cash on a Michelin-starred salad.
- The sarcastic suspect either ate the cheeseburger or the margherita pizza.
- The blue-eyed suspect is intolerant to dairy products.
- No, the polite suspect is not single. Sorry lads.
- Romance is complicated for the ambitious career woman.
- **The million pounds of alimony will not be spent on a baby.**

		LAST MEAL				FOOD INTOLERANCE				RELATIONSHIP			
		Cheeseburger	Margherita Pizza	Penne Arrabiata	Salade Niçoise	Dairy	Onion	Tomato	Wheat	Complicated	Divorced	Married	Single
SUSPECTS	Emma Bidet												
	Kate Colon												
	Lisa Bogroll												
	Megan McTurdy												
RELATIONSHIP	Complicated												
	Divorced												
	Married												
	Single												
FOOD INTOLERANCE	Dairy												
	Onion												
	Tomato												
	Wheat												

WHAT IS THEIR RELATIONSHIP STATUS?

WHICH FOOD DISAGREES WITH THEM?

WHO IS NOT PREGNANT?

WHAT DID THEY LAST EAT?

Suspects	Relationship Status	Food Intolerance	Last Meal
Emma Bidet			
Kate Colon			
Lisa Bogroll			
Megan McTurdy			

3. BUTTHOLE IN ONE

Inspector Poupe goes to the links at St. Anne-Poos for a bit of golf. Partway through the second round, play is suspended. One of the players desperately needed the toilet, but they didn't want to cause disruption. Rather than forfeit, they defecated on the course.

Poupe matches each player to their current club, where they were when the turd was discovered and what they had scored on the previous hole.

SUSPECTS

A young fellow from Luxembourg who often squires for the other golfers. Today, he's representing himself.

5'6" – CAP – WINS: 6

A gross old man who wipes his snot on the outside lapels of his coat.

6'1" – MUTTON CHOPS – WINS: 18

An eccentric who forages between rounds. Some people claim to have seen him eating grass, and it would explain his green turds.

5'11" – BEARDED – WINS: 56

The reigning champion. He always places himself upwind of the other golfers so his smell will put them off their game.

6'0" – SHORT HAIR – WINS: 82

LOCATION

Bunker

Sand-filled, so you could easily bury a turd.

Fairway

Well-maintained grass that makes up the majority of the course.

Green

The smooth, short grass surrounding the hole.

Rough

The thick, bristly grass on the edge of the course.

SCORE

Birdie

One stroke below par – maybe the first-ever birdie hit a bird mid-flight.

Bogey

One stroke over par. Could have been named for Colonel Bogey, who scores this more often than not.

Eagle

The king of birds is a score of two under par.

Par

The number of strokes an average golfer needs to get their ball in the hole.

CLUB

Iron	Putter
May be used to smooth one's clothes between rounds.	A gentle tap from the putter is all that's needed once you're on the green.

Wedge	Wood
A special club for getting your balls out of sticky situations.	A stiff club which can send the ball further than any other.

CLUES

- The man with mutton chops surprised himself by achieving a par score on the previous hole.
- Whoever was on the green when play was suspended had birdied the previous hole.
- The golfer with the lowest number of career wins wasn't in the bunker when the dump was found.
- The golfer currently using the wood scored two under par on the previous hole – impressive!
- Inspector Poupe's favourite golfer is holding either the putter or the wedge. (See Exhibit B.)
- The bearded golfer scored one under par on the previous hole – not too shabby!
- The bogey wasn't scored by the golfer now holding a putter.
- Someone was using an iron on the fairway when the turd was discovered.
- **The secret shitter is holding a putter.**

		CLUB				SCORE				LOCATION		
	Iron	Putter	Wedge	Wood	Birdie	Bogey	Eagle	Par	Bunker	Fairway	Green	Rough
SUSPECTS: Caddie Flicht												
Colonel Bogey												
Graham Garlick												
Will Whiffgift												
LOCATION: Bunker												
Fairway												
Green												
Rough												
SCORE: Birdie												
Bogey												
Eagle												
Par												

WHERE WERE THEY?

WHAT HAD THEY SCORED ON THE PREVIOUS HOLE?

WHO DID THE POO?

WHAT CLUB WERE THEY USING?

Suspects	Location	Score	Club
Caddie Flicht			
Colonel Bogey			
Graham Garlick			
Will Whiffgift			

4. WHO-DUNG-IT?

A steward's enquiry has been launched at Poomarket after outrage in the parade ring. One of the horses has defecated on the ground and the chief steward has put his foot in it, literally. Outraged by having 'poo shoe', the steward makes the entirely rational decision to ban the offending horse from the race as punishment. Inspector Poupe, something of a horse-racing connoisseur, is at the racecourse today and immediately offers his services to the irate steward. He soon deduces the favourite racecourse of each horse, its rider and racing colours, enabling him to work out who-dung-it.

SUSPECTS

Bronx Cheer

This powerful stallion is named because he passes a prodigious amount of wind that sounds just like a Bronx Cheer.

AGE 3 – BLACK – HEIGHT 159 CM

Stool Time

This pedigree animal is fed a high-calorie diet to provide it with all the energy it needs to run fast. Also creates a lot of manure for the local farmer.

AGE 2 – CHESTNUT – HEIGHT 162 CM

Tinkle Toes

This graceful mare is very light on her feet. Wees more than any horse known to man, so the name was an obvious choice.

AGE 5 – ROAN – HEIGHT 157 CM

Top Scat

He's the alpha male of the group, and marks his territory by producing the smelliest dung of them all.

AGE 7 – GREY – HEIGHT 170 CM

FAVOURITE RACECOURSE

Asscot

One horse won the prestigious Gold Crap at Asscot – surely the highlight of any horse's career.

Fartwell Park

Set in stunning scenery, one horse put the 'ass' in 'Classic' when they farted all the way through their winning run in the iconic Fartwell Classic.

Poomarket

Despite also holding fond memories of winning the Grim National at Paintree, one horse's favourite racecourse will always be Poomarket. Nothing will ever top the day it won the Maiden Handicrap event in its first-ever race.

Ripoon

One horse gets the shakes whenever it thinks about Ripoon, where it famously beat Red Bum in a finish line thriller in the Brown Ring Stakes.

JOCKEY

Brenda Bridle

A lifetime's bending over has given Brenda Bridle a sore back and an even sorer bottom.

Clive Canter

A former stable lad, he's smelt more than his fair share of horseshit in his life.

Gary Gallop

A good jockey, but infamous for *that* fall at Paintree where he landed on his arse and had to have reconstructive surgery to the butt cheeks. Now he has a very dire rear.

Will Whip

The most competitive jockey currently racing, this guy loves to hold the whip hand over his fellow jockeys. A big talker, he's also full of shit.

Beige

One jockey has silks in this dull sandy colour, reminiscent of an oatmeal-coloured poo.

Brown Sleeves

Let's hope the brown sleeves are part of the design and the jockey didn't get caught short of loo roll when having their traditional pre-race poo.

Chocolate Hoops

Mmm... chocolate. But was the jockey sitting on a horse that was secretly creating its own chocolate treat?

Dark Brown Spots

Were the brown spots meant to be there, or were they caused by a chronic case of splashback?

CLUES

- The grey horse's favourite racecourse is the venue that hosts the prestigious Gold Crap event.
- The jockey with a sore back (and bottom) is on board the horse that loves Fartwell Park.
- The graceful mare loves Ripoon.
- The jockey riding the three-year-old is either a former stable lad or the most competitive jockey.
- Will Whip wouldn't wear a colour as dull as beige.
- The jockey with a dire rear is sporting dark brown spots today.
- Will Whip has never ridden Top Scat.
- The horse that loves Asscot above all other courses is being ridden by a jockey wearing silks festooned with chocolate hoops.
- **The dung on the steward's shoe was produced by the winner of the Maiden Handicrap.**

		RACING COLOURS				JOCKEY				RACECOURSE			
		Beige	Brown Sleeves	Chocolate Hoops	Dark Brown Spots	Brenda Bridle	Clive Canter	Gary Gallop	Will Whip	Asscot	Fartwell Park	Poomarket	Ripoon
SUSPECTS	Bronx Cheer												
	Stool Time												
	Tinkle Toes												
	Top Scat												
RACECOURSE	Asscot												
	Fartwell Park												
	Poomarket												
	Ripoon												
JOCKEY	Brenda Bridle												
	Clive Canter												
	Gary Gallop												
	Will Whip												

WHAT'S THEIR FAVOURITE RACECOURSE?

WHO'S THE JOCKEY?

WHICH HORSE DID THE POO?

WHAT ARE THE RACING COLOURS?

Suspects	Favourite Racecourse	Jockey	Racing Colours
Bronx Cheer			
Stool Time			
Tinkle Toes			
Top Scat			

5. SERIAL POOER

The peaceful neighbourhood of Juniper Bottom is being terrorised by a serial pooer. Revolting stools are appearing all over the village, wreaking havoc and just generally reeking. Determined to get to the bottom of this, Inspector Poupe narrows down his suspects to four local stinkballs. He susses out their possible motives, the character of their stools and where they were at the time of the last incident.

SUSPECTS

Mickey Bumholes

The local butcher, widely regarded as a complete oddball with worrying access to sharp knives.

6'2" – BLUE EYES – SMELLS OF BUMHOLES

Mucky Mel

The local baker. Her personal hygiene might be questionable but her iced buns are delicious!

5'8" – GREEN EYES – SMELLS OF SWEAT

Pongy Paul

The town postie. He seems a nice enough chap as long as you keep your distance.

5'9" – BROWN EYES – SMELLS OF FISH

Rancid Rachel

A talented hairdresser whom clients will happily hold their breath for.

5'6" – HAZEL EYES – SMELLS OF SICK

LOCATION

Garden Centre

Famously sells huge bags of crap.

Library

A cultural hub, the shelves are heaving with classics – *The Great Shatsby*, *Middlefarts* and *Wuthering Shites* to name but a few.

Playground

Complete with all the Ss: sandpits, swings, slides and... shit?

Supermarket

Could there be another clean-up on aisle 3?

MOTIVE

A Prank

Just some mischievous, scatological fun.

Cruelty

Just pure, senseless cruelty.

Desperation

When nature calls, it's time to answer.

Revenge

A dish best served cold, unlike these steaming hot turds.

STOOL TYPE

Enormous Not far off the size of a baby's head.	**Fluffy** Not as cute as it sounds.
Runny Perfect for producing maximum levels of mess.	**Sausage-like** Looks like a sausage, but certainly won't taste like one.

CLUES

- Rancid Rachel would only do a public poo out of sheer desperation.
- The butcher squirts out runny stools.
- The sausage-pooer was reading a copy of *Middlefarts*.
- The producer of enormous poos was at the garden centre.
- The tallest suspect is not allowed near playgrounds.
- The town postie was either shopping for food or pushing his kids on the swings.
- The poo that is not as cute as it sounds was produced by someone motivated by revenge.
- The sausage-like poo is the proud creation of someone seeking mischievous scatological fun.
- **The phantom pooer was motivated by cruelty.**

		STOOL TYPE				MOTIVE				LOCATION			
		Enormous	Fluffy	Runny	Sausage-like	A Prank	Cruelty	Desperation	Revenge	Garden Centre	Library	Playground	Supermarket
SUSPECTS	Mickey Bumholes												
	Mucky Mel												
	Pongy Paul												
	Rancid Rachel												
LOCATION	Garden Centre												
	Library												
	Playground												
	Supermarket												
MOTIVE	A Prank												
	Cruelty												
	Desperation												
	Revenge												

WHERE DID THEY LAST POO?

WHAT WAS THEIR MOTIVE?

WHO IS THE SERIAL POOER?

WHAT ARE THEIR STOOLS LIKE?

Suspects	Location	Motive	Stool Type
Mickey Bumholes			
Mucky Mel			
Pongy Paul			
Rancid Rachel			

6. TOP OF THE POOPS

Welcome to *Top Of The Poops*, the show that celebrates number ones and number twos! The programme has seen its fair share of divas and difficult musicians, but nothing has caused the audience to wrinkle their noses quite like the foul stench which filled the studio last Thursday evening. Inspector Poupe soon arrived on the scene and promptly announced that someone had clearly soiled themselves. He works out which musician caused the stink, what instrument they play, their hit song and which band they are in.

SUSPECTS

Ava Hole

An ethereal Swedish musician taking the world by shitstorm. Her hits include 'I Will Always Love Poo' and 'Oops... I Did Shit Again'.

5'6" – STOCKHOLM – AGE 23

Billy Pumps

He's a classic heart-throb. Pumpmania has truly swept the land.

6'0" – BOSTON – AGE 32

Sid Chunks

He once came first in a celebrity lookalike competition and still brags about it to this day.

5'9" – CARDIFF – AGE 26

Zoe Wee

A cool customer. Dresses head-to-toe in black. Lives off cigarettes and adrenaline.

5'4" – CHICAGO – AGE 33

INSTRUMENT

Bass

Its low-frequency vibrations have been known to induce bowel movements.

Drums

So easy a monkey could do it.

Keyboard

Impress your friends by putting it in demo mode and pretending to play.

Lead Guitar

Just learn four chords and riff the rest. Easy!

BAND

Electric Turd

A compelling blend of turd-wave punk and experimental wazz.

Stall Rockers

A groovy modern take on classic rock 'n' roll.

The Splash

An anarcho-indie-disco extravaganza.

Touching Cloth

Pioneered an irreverent fusion of gospel and heavy metal.

SONG

'Brown River'	'I Want Poo'
Featuring an iconic guitar solo.	An unshakeable earworm, you'll be singing it all day long.
'In the Groove'	**'Your Pong'**
The number one wiping anthem.	A sentimental ballad on how true love is tolerating each other's smells.

CLUES

- The tallest musician performed a dazzling rendition of 'I Want Poo'.
- The Swedish musician plays the drums.
- The Stall Rockers rose up the charts with their best-selling single, 'Your Pong'.
- The youngest musician either performed with Electric Turd or Touching Cloth.
- The winner of the celebrity lookalike competition is on bass.
- The musician who has mastered four chords with aplomb performed 'Brown River'.
- The Splash performed their number two hit, 'I Want Poo'.
- The musician from Chicago is not a member of Electric Turd.
- **The smell of poo arose to the iconic sound of anarcho-indie-disco music.**

		SONG				BAND				INSTRUMENT			
		Brown River	I Want Poo	In the Groove	Your Pong	Electric Turd	Stall Rockers	The Splash	Touching Cloth	Bass	Drums	Keyboard	Lead Guitar
SUSPECTS	Ava Hole												
	Billy Pumps												
	Sid Chunks												
	Zoe Wee												
INSTRUMENT	Bass												
	Drums												
	Keyboard												
	Lead Guitar												
BAND	Electric Turd												
	Stall Rockers												
	The Splash												
	Touching Cloth												

WHAT DO THEY PLAY?

WHAT BAND ARE THEY IN?

WHO DID THE POO?

WHAT SONG DID THEY PERFORM?

Suspects	Instrument	Band	Song
Ava Hole			
Billy Pumps			
Sid Chunks			
Zoe Wee			

7. THE INCRUDIBLES

With great 'pooer', they say, comes great responsibility. One of these superheroes hasn't been very responsible: while battling their nemesis, they dropped a fat turd, and they didn't stop to clean it up. Poupe is called in to bring the offender to justice. He works out which superhero did the super-poo, what their superpower is and their nemesis's name and evil plan.

SUSPECTS

Incontinent Isaiah

An elderly superhero who's been pulled out of retirement to face a new generation of supervillains. He may not be able to control his bladder, but he can still show those whippersnappers who's boss.

5'6" – BALD – AGE 81

Miss Mist

A German superhero with a potty mouth. She works alone, not by choice.

5'7" – BLONDE HAIR – AGE 27

Pooperman

Is it a turd? Yes. It's Pooperman.

6'4" – BROWN HAIR – AGE 31

Skunk-Man

Smells so bad that many people think it's his superpower, but no: he was born that way.

5'9" – BLACK HAIR WITH A WHITE STRIPE – AGE 24

SUPERPOWERS

Pyrokinesis

The ability to shoot fire.
Out of the mouth, right?

Super Strength

The sheer force of their bowel movements has been known to crack toilets in half.

Telekinesis

Telekines can manipulate objects with their minds. Yes, they can wipe without hands.

Telepathy

A telepath can read minds, so don't try to let out a silent one nearby. You won't get away with it.

NEMESIS

Kami-Khazi

His name means 'divine toilet', or so I'm told.

Loocifer

A cocky young supervillain who aspires to rule the world.

Porcellana

Also known as 'the White Queen', she wears a dress made of polished porcelain.

The Turdinator

Half man, half toilet, the Turdinator is one of humanity's most fearsome foes.

EVIL PLAN

Block The Sewers	Hack Into Your Toilet
And make the drains overflow. Bring a spare pair of socks, because it's going to get messy.	This supervillain wants to replace all toilets with e-toilets and steal the shape of your behind.
Prevent Litter Collection	**Pump Sewage Into The Ocean**
Maybe once we realise how much we throw away, we'll be more responsible, right? Right?	Well, pump *more* sewage than usual.

CLUES

- The fiendish Porcellana intends to pump sewage into the ocean. Her partner in crime, Loocifer, wants to block the sewers and make the drains overflow. Mwah ha ha.
- The Turdinator is the nemesis of the superhero with super strength.
- The 5'9" superhero is either a telepath or a telekine. Nobody wants to get close enough to find out.
- The oldest superhero has sworn to defeat the villain who wears brown-tinted glasses (see Exhibit B).
- The superhero with pyrokinetic powers is trying to stop one of these supervillains from hacking into the world's toilet network.
- The tallest superhero's nemesis is not the dreadful Turdinator.
- The telekinetic superhero hasn't been fighting the villain who wants to flood the ocean with sewage.
- **The superhero who did the poo has cracked toilets in half.**

	EVIL PLAN: Block The Sewers	EVIL PLAN: Hack Into Your Toilet	EVIL PLAN: Prevent Litter Collection	EVIL PLAN: Pump Sewage Into The Ocean	NEMESIS: Kami-Khazi	NEMESIS: Loocifer	NEMESIS: Porcellana	NEMESIS: The Turdinator	SUPERPOWERS: Pyrokinesis	SUPERPOWERS: Super Strength	SUPERPOWERS: Telekinesis	SUPERPOWERS: Telepathy
SUSPECTS: Incontinent Isaiah												
SUSPECTS: Miss Mist												
SUSPECTS: Pooperman												
SUSPECTS: Skunk-Man												
SUPERPOWERS: Pyrokinesis												
SUPERPOWERS: Super Strength												
SUPERPOWERS: Telekinesis												
SUPERPOWERS: Telepathy												
NEMESIS: Kami-Khazi												
NEMESIS: Loocifer												
NEMESIS: Porcellana												
NEMESIS: The Turdinator												

WHAT IS THEIR SUPERPOWER?

WHO IS THEIR NEMESIS?

WHO DID THE POO?

WHAT IS THEIR NEMESIS'S EVIL PLAN?

Suspects	Superpowers	Nemesis	Evil Plan
Incontinent Isaiah			
Miss Mist			
Pooperman			
Skunk-Man			

8. ANCIENT POO

Four archaeologists are out on digs when one makes an unexpected discovery. Having uncovered a fascinating artefact, they can't help but poo their pants in delight. Inspector Poupe is intrigued when he receives the call to investigate and find the culprit. He soon discovers which archaeologist did the poo, which artefact they found, where they were digging and what tool they used.

SUSPECTS

Dr. Dumps

An archaeologist of some considerable repute, she takes a special interest in the diets of ancient people.

5'4" – SWISS – AGE 58

Lady Logs

Her claim to fame is discovering the tomb of Sagremor the Smelly which, let's be honest, can't have been hard.

5'2" – ENGLISH – AGE 49

Professor Squits

Boasts of a long and illustrious career scrabbling around in the dirt.

5'7" – GERMAN – AGE 62

Sir Poopster

An ex-military man. He's hard as nails, unlike these other academics.

6'1" – SCOTTISH – AGE 46

LOCATION

Beach

All sorts of discoveries are revealed by the waves.

Field

Some believe it may be the site of an Iron Age lavatory.

Hillside

Covered in sheep droppings, and maybe some human excrement too?

Woodland

Contains a high density of wildlife and therefore poo.

TOOL

Pitchfork

Doubles up as a handy tool for joining angry mobs.

Shovel

Perfect for shovelling shit.

Spade

With a steel blade to cut through compacted earth.

Trowel

Use this while squatting in the trench.

ARTEFACT

Arrowhead	Coin
Rusted to an unappealing shade of brown.	An ancient Roman Pooparius, to be exact.
Jewellery	**Pottery Shards**
A craft as old as shit itself.	Suspected of belonging to an old chamberpot.

CLUES

- The Swiss archaeologist went digging at the beach.
- The 49 year old excavated the woodland.
- The steel blade unearthed a piece of jewellery.
- The 5'4" archaeologist had a pitchfork and a shovel to choose from.
- An Iron Age arrowhead was found in the field.
- Sir Poopster was using his tool of choice while squatting in a trench.
- No shovels were used in the woodland.
- The English archaeologist gave their find to Inspector Poupe (see Exhibit B).
- **The pottery was pants-pooingly exciting.**

	ARTEFACT				TOOL				LOCATION			
	Arrowhead	Coin	Jewellery	Pottery Shards	Pitchfork	Shovel	Spade	Trowel	Beach	Field	Hillside	Woodland
SUSPECTS												
Dr. Dumps												
Lady Logs												
Professor Squits												
Sir Poopster												
LOCATION												
Beach												
Field												
Hillside												
Woodland												
TOOL												
Pitchfork												
Shovel												
Spade												
Trowel												

WHERE WERE THEY EXCAVATING?

WHAT TOOL WERE THEY DIGGING WITH?

WHO DID THE POO?

WHAT ARTEFACT DID THEY FIND?

Suspects	Location	Tool	Artefact
Dr. Dumps			
Lady Logs			
Professor Squits			
Sir Poopster			

9. TURD OF THE TIDE

Most of us will have urinated in the sea at some point in our lives. What about having a poo?

In this troubling case, somebody took a clandestine crap on the beach, then hid the evidence under a sandcastle. Yet the truth will out no matter how strenuously we seek to hide it: when the tide came in, the shit was seen bobbing among the waves.

Where did this occur, what was the sandcastle like, what material was it made of and who was the culprit? Inspector Poupe investigates...

SUSPECTS

Betty Bowles

Betty gets to the beach early to spread her towel. Did she take advantage of the empty sands to pinch a loaf?

5'5" – BARE HEAD – AGE 19

John Quincy

An American tourist in the UK, he's relieved to be somewhere where people don't laugh at his name.

5'10" – COWBOY HAT – AGE 28

Kathryn Krapper

A lazy undergraduate who would rather go to the beach than study. Could she be bothered to walk to the toilets?

5'9" – BOBBLE HAT – AGE 21

Malcolm Moreshit

An architect's apprentice, Malcolm practises by building sandcastles. Is human faeces an efficient substitute for cement?

5'11" – FLAT CAP – AGE 23

LOCATION

Gryme Regis

A Dorset town renowned for the fossil coprolites found on its beaches.

Robin Hood's Bog

A beautiful Yorkshire town once used as a latrine by Robin Hood and his merry men.

Shitby

Another Yorkshire town, this one a former whaling hotspot. It's much nicer than the name suggests.

Wastings

A town in Sussex where a king died after getting a fleck of shit in his eye.

SANDCASTLE TYPE

Fancy

Made in one of those fancy castle-shaped buckets. Cocktail umbrellas have been stuck in the turrets.

Heaped

Just a heap of sand, no defences.

Moated

A deep moat surrounds the citadel of this sandcastle. It won't stop the sea for long.

Walled

The builder has surrounded himself with a compact wall of sand while he waits for the tide to come in.

SAND TYPE

Dry Sand

Not an ideal building material, since it blows away.

Mud

River mud, sticky and gross.

Shingle

Sand made of larger, stonier granules. Can still be used to build, although it doesn't stick together well.

Wet Sand

Every sandcastle expert knows wet is best.

CLUES

- The American was either visiting Gryme Regis or Wastings.
- Shitby beach is shingly.
- The sandcastle in Robin Hood's Bog was a mere heap.
- In Dorset, no one built a sandcastle out of mud.
- The walled sandcastle wasn't constructed out of wet sand.
- The sandcastle in the former whaling hotspot was surrounded by a moat.
- The woman in the bobble hat built with dry sand.
- The architect's apprentice decorated his castle with cocktail umbrellas.
- **Until the tide came in, the sandcastle the turd was under was made of dry sand.**

		SAND TYPE				SANDCASLTE TYPE				LOCATION			
		Dry Sand	Mud	Shingle	Wet Sand	Fancy	Heaped	Moated	Walled	Gryme Regis	Robin Hood's Bog	Shitby	Wastings
SUSPECTS	Betty Bowles												
	John Quincy												
	Kathryn Krapper												
	Malcolm Moreshit												
LOCATION	Gryme Regis												
	Robin Hood's Bog												
	Shitby												
	Wastings												
SANDCASLTE TYPE	Fancy												
	Heaped												
	Moated												
	Walled												

WHERE WERE THEY?

WHAT TYPE OF SANDCASTLE DID THEY MAKE?

WHO BURIED THE POO?

WHAT TYPE OF SAND DID THEY USE?

Suspects	Location	Sandcastle Type	Sand Type
Betty Bowles			
John Quincy			
Kathryn Krapper			
Malcolm Moreshit			

10. REST AND RE-LAX

Inspector Poupe is conducting a paid experiment on laxatives. He's hired four poor sufferers of constipation and fed them each a home remedy. He then sits back and waits for the explosions to begin.

However, reviewing his data, Poupe realises that one of his test subjects was faking it and only there for the money. He matches each participant to the food they ate, the reason they gave for being constipated and the number of times they flushed to work out who ruined his experiment. Back to the drawing board!

SUSPECTS

Blocked-Up Barbara

Has suffered from constipation for most of her adult life. Poupe's advert is a godsend.

5'7" – WEARING RED – AGE 43

Can't-Shit Sally

The nickname was given to her by friends tired of having to wait outside the toilet door.

5'6" – WEARING BLUE – AGE 37

Costive Connor

'Costive' is a fancy way of saying constipated, and Connor is a fancy man.

5'11" – WEARING YELLOW – AGE 32

No-Dung Norbert

He eats very little, but he still gets constipated. It's a hard life.

5'10" – WEARING GREEN – AGE 50

FOOD

Chocolate Milk

Diarrhoea in a bottle.

Jar Of Prunes

A traditional constipation remedy. Eat with care.

Probiotic Yoghurt

Yoghurt infested with microorganisms. Yummy.

Rhubarb Crumble

Just like grandmother used to make.

REASON

Dehydration

If you don't drink enough water, your stools will harden and wedge.

Held It In

Sometimes you gotta go, but it's not the time or place.

Not Enough Fibre

A bowl of porridge should help, or some bran.

Sitting Down Too Much

Sitting down for long periods of time can cause constipation.

TIMES FLUSHED

1	2
A single, simple flush.	Two flushes is just about socially acceptable to dispose of a persistent stool.
3	**4**
If anyone's waiting outside the door, they're now judging you.	FOUR? What are you trying to flush, Mount Everest?

CLUES

- The woman in blue didn't flush three times. She'd eaten Poupe's grandmother's rhubarb crumble.
- The person who consumed 'diarrhoea in a bottle' flushed on the second attempt.
- The oldest person flushed more than two times. A large turd, theirs.
- The person wearing red sits in a chair all day, and that's why they're constipated. They flushed once.
- Rhubarb crumble wasn't eaten by the person suffering from dehydration.
- The person that held it in ate a jar of prunes with gusto – there's no better way to loosen your bowels.
- **The faker's turd smelt like old yoghurt.**

	TIMES FLUSHED 1	2	3	4	REASON Dehydration	Held It In	Not Enough Fibre	Sitting Down Too Much	FOOD Chocolate Milk	Jar Of Prunes	Probiotic Yoghurt	Rhubarb Crumble
SUSPECTS Blocked-Up Barbara												
Can't-Shit Sally												
Costive Connor												
No-Dung Norbert												
FOOD Chocolate Milk												
Jar Of Prunes												
Probiotic Yoghurt												
Rhubarb Crumble												
REASON Dehydration												
Held It In												
Not Enough Fibre												
Sitting Down Too Much												

WHAT DID THEY EAT?

WHY DID THEY CLAIM TO BE CONSTIPATED?

WHO'S JUST THERE FOR THE MONEY?

HOW MANY TIMES DID THEY FLUSH?

Suspects	Food	Reason	Times Flushed
Blocked-Up Barbara			
Can't-Shit Sally			
Costive Connor			
No-Dung Norbert			

11. CLOSE ENCOUNTERS OF THE TURD KIND

Aliens walk among us... and they shit among us, too. Inspector Poupe is approached by men in black, who take him to a top-secret research facility on extraterrestrial intelligence. There, Poupe's world is turned upside down. He learns that alien tourists are permitted to enter Earth, but leaving their refuse is a violation of the intergalactic directive against littering. The Government requests his expertise to work out which type of alien broke the law, how they arrived, what they'd eaten and the shape the stool was.

SUSPECTS

Grey

Wise, inscrutable beings with enormous craniums. For all their wisdom, they haven't managed to eliminate the need to defecate.

5'4" – GREY – CURIOUS

Little Green Man

Small, green and mean crap-machines.

4'0" – GREEN – ILL-TEMPERED

Reptilian

Frightening scaled creatures who ruled Earth aeons ago, and look forward to the time when they shall do so again.

6'7" – BEIGE – LAZY

Space Bug

Many-eyed monstrosities from the voids of space. They have a tendency to drool.

6'1" – PURPLE – HUNGRY

ARRIVED BY

Crashed Spaceship

Even hi-tech alien technology can fail. Stand well back when it does.

Flying Saucer

Because flying cups aren't aerodynamic.

Meteor

Do not investigate the crash site. Have you never seen a sci-fi movie?

Teleportation

Very snazzy, but there's always a risk of appearing inside a wall.

FOOD

Freeze-Dried Ice Cream

A favourite snack of astronauts, who have passed the taste on to aliens. Usually strawberry, vanilla and chocolate.

Hamburger

The pinnacle of human civilisation, according to some.

Turkey

Poor turkeys. Not only do they look weird, but apparently both humans AND aliens love eating them.

Vegetables

Some aliens have evolved beyond uncivilised humanity and no longer consume meat. It doesn't do the smell of their dung any favours.

STOOL SHAPE

Cube	Log
Those sharp vertices must be painful to pass, but maybe aliens have reinforced colons.	An ordinary turd by human standards.

Sphere	Torus
You could play bowls with this if you wore gloves.	A perfect doughnut symbolising infinity. It also stinks.

CLUES

- The alien in the flying saucer had a ravenous desire for turkey.
- The beige alien crawled out of a shattered meteor. Its faeces were shaped either like a log or a torus.
- The prodigious intelligence of the Grey craved frozen ice cream.
- This clue has been written in alien hieroglyphics – see Exhibit B.
- The purple alien has spherical stools.
- The teleporting alien did not visit Earth to consume a food item some consider to be the pinnacle of human civilisation. Whichever alien did eat that food item had a cubic crap shortly afterwards.
- **The poo that wasn't cleaned up was shaped like a torus.**

		Cube	Log	Sphere	Torus	Freeze-Dried Ice Cream	Hamburger	Turkey	Vegetables	Crashed Spaceship	Flying Saucer	Meteor	Teleportation
		STOOL SHAPE				FOOD				ARRIVED BY			
SUSPECTS	Grey												
	Little Green Man												
	Reptilian												
	Space Bug												
ARRIVED BY	Crashed Spaceship												
	Flying Saucer												
	Meteor												
	Teleportation												
FOOD	Freeze-Dried Ice Cream												
	Hamburger												
	Turkey												
	Vegetables												

HOW DID THEY ARRIVE?

WHAT HAD THEY EATEN?

WHICH ALIEN DID THE POO?

WHAT SHAPE WAS THE STOOL?

Suspects	Arrived By	Food	Stool Shape
Grey			
Little Green Man			
Reptilian			
Space Bug			

12. THE SYMPOOSIUM

Inspector Poupe attends an academic conference to hear his father read a paper. After hours of mind-numbing boredom, he perks up when the organisers announce that a mysterious lump of excrement has been discovered near the disco. Finally, something he specialises in! The Inspector matches these four suspicious scholars to their subject and what they ate and drank during the conference. Who's getting the sack?

SUSPECTS

Bea Esse

Beatrice Esse is an up-and-coming scholar who has never falsified her data. At least, she says so, and someone who's never falsified their data can be trusted, can't they?

AGE 25 – DOCTORAL STUDENT – WEARS BROWN

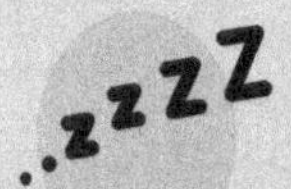

Dr. Drivel

When he takes to the podium, the audience falls asleep in self-defence.

AGE 54 – DOCTOR – WEARS GREY

Fulla Schitt

A doctoral student known for asking probing questions at conferences.

AGE 24 – DOCTORAL STUDENT – WEARS BLACK

Professor Poupe

Inspector Poupe's father, a distinguished academic. He disapproves of his son's 'frivolous' career.

AGE 62 – PROFESSOR – WEARS TWEEDS

SUBJECT

Anthropoology

Did you know that the Romans wiped with sponges, and that in some cultures the toilet connects to a pigsty? If not, you evidently haven't met an anthropoologist. They can talk the arse end off a donkey.

Episstemology

Episstemologists ask questions about knowledge, such as: if a bear shits in the woods and nobody's around to see the turd fall, did it really happen?

Escatology

Not to be confused with eschatology, which is a branch of theology dealing with the end of the world.

Shiterary Theory

The study of famous scatological texts throughout history, such as this one.

FOOD

Cocktail Sausage

It's impossible to eat just one.

Potato Salad

Sprinkled with chives and drizzled with mayonnaise.

Scotch Egg

A boiled egg encased in pork encased in breadcrumbs. Scrumptious.

Tempura

Shrimp deep-fried until it's golden. A Japanese dish.

DRINK

Champagne	Red Wine
If the university is paying, you might as well splurge.	Red as blood, red as rubies, red as... er... tomatoes.
Water	**White Wine**
It's wisest to stay sober at a conference. Remember: you're among colleagues, not friends.	A cheap white wine that's halfway to becoming vinegar.

CLUES

- The father of our esteemed protagonist helped himself to a handful of cocktail sausages.
- The shiterary theorist delighted in a plate of tempura.
- The man in grey specialises in anthropoology.
- By the end of the conference, Fulla Schitt was also full of white wine.
- A Scotch egg with a glass of red wine is an unconventional pairing, but it worked for one of these academics.
- The tweed-wearer doesn't study episstemology. The escatologist didn't drink water.
- Dr. Drivel either drank champagne or water.
- **The shit was flecked with half-digested chives.**

		DRINK			FOOD				SUBJECT			
	Champagne	Red Wine	Water	White Wine	Cocktail Sausage	Potato Salad	Scotch Egg	Tempura	Anthropoology	Episstemology	Escatology	Shiterary Theory
SUSPECTS: Bea Esse												
Dr. Drivel												
Fulla Schitt												
Professor Poupe												
SUBJECT: Anthropoology												
Episstemology												
Escatology												
Shiterary Theory												
FOOD: Cocktail Sausage												
Potato Salad												
Scotch Egg												
Tempura												

WHAT'S THEIR SUBJECT?

WHAT DID THEY EAT?

WHO DID THE POO?

WHAT DID THEY DRINK?

Suspects	Subject	Food	Drink
Bea Esse			
Dr. Drivel			
Fulla Schitt			
Professor Poupe			

13. PEST IN SHOW

These four pampered pet pooches have been entered into a dog show by their besotted owners. However, as the award ceremony begins, the judges have made a shocking discovery – a steaming dog poo. They determine the culprit will be disqualified on hygiene grounds. But how to find out who did it? It's another case for the intrepid Inspector Poupe, of course, and he immediately sets to work matching the dogs to their breed, the category they entered and where they were when the doo-doo was discovered. The judges have faith in Poupe. When he points the finger, you can be sure he won't be barking up the wrong tree.

SUSPECTS

Angel

Angel by name, yes, but also by nature? That's for you to determine.

AGE 6 MONTHS – HEIGHT 55 CM – BLUE COLLAR

Buddy

Buddy is described by his owner as a loyal and faithful friend. Hopefully he didn't break that loyalty by doing the poo.

AGE 24 MONTHS – HEIGHT 60 CM – RED COLLAR

Karma

The name is not what you think. Her owner has another dog who is much more excitable, whereas Karma is calmer, hence the name.

AGE 18 MONTHS – HEIGHT 25 CM – BROWN COLLAR

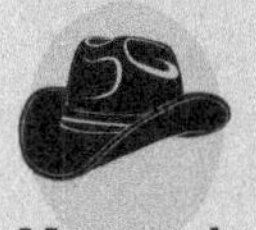

Maverick

An extremely independent-minded dog, it would be in his nature to take a dump just when he wasn't supposed to. But that doesn't mean he did.

AGE 12 MONTHS – HEIGHT 50 CM – BLUE COLLAR

LOCATION

Balance Beam

A dicey place to do your business. Lose your balance and it'll be a shitshow.

Hurdle

A mid-air turd? Maybe that would be strangely liberating, but surely it wouldn't go unnoticed.

Podium

Only the most thrill-seeking of dogs would drop a turd just as they were being given an award.

Tunnel

A great place to do a poo – no pesky humans watching you do it. Plausible deniability is no problem here.

BREED

German Shepturd

A medium-to-large breed of dog, named for its distinctively stinky poo.

Lavrador

A friendly and energetic dog breed. According to urban legend, one clever individual once learned to use a real toilet, hence the name.

Poodle

A breed of water dog that literally has 'poo' in its name. Did our poodle live up to its name today?

Shit tzu

The breed is said to have been bred from the Pookingese and the Lhasa Apoo. After that crossing, the name was a bit of a no-brainer.

CATEGORY ENTERED

Best Trick

Whether it's giving a kiss, rolling over or bowing, there are lots of tricks that can be performed. The dog that did the turd would be well advised to play dead.

Cutest Eyes

Who can resist those puppy dog eyes? Well, it's easier if there's an aroma of poo in the air.

Nicest Coat

The nicest coat is one that provides warmth, protection and comfort. It doesn't refer to a natty orange anorak.

Waggiest Tail

Measured in wags per second, presumably the higher the better.

CLUES

- The breed named for its distinctively smelly poo was by the podium when the judges made their unwanted discovery.
- The shit tzu got her name because her owner thought she was (relatively) calm.
- The one-year-old dog was entered in either the best trick or waggiest tail category.
- The dog with the angelic name was standing by the hurdle, but was not trying to win the waggiest tail category.
- The poodle is 50 cm tall.
- The dog standing by the balance beam was entered into the cutest eyes category.
- The poodle is not in the running for the waggiest tail award.
- **The cutest eyes entrant was the guilty poo-ch.**

		CATEGORY ENTERED				BREED				LOCATION			
		Best Trick	Cutest Eyes	Nicest Coat	Waggiest Tail	German Shepturd	Lavrador	Poodle	Shit tzu	Balance Beam	Hurdle	Podium	Tunnel
SUSPECTS	Angel												
	Buddy												
	Karma												
	Maverick												
LOCATION	Balance Beam												
	Hurdle												
	Podium												
	Tunnel												
BREED	German Shepturd												
	Lavrador												
	Poodle												
	Shit tzu												

WHERE DID THEY DO IT?

WHAT BREED ARE THEY?

WHICH DOG DID THE TURD?

WHICH CATEGORY HAD THEY ENTERED?

Suspects	Location	Breed	Category Entered
Angel			
Buddy			
Karma			
Maverick			

14. TOO HOT TO HANDLE

On his evening off, Inspector Poupe goes for a curry at his favourite curry house. At the next table are a group of friends, all giving it large about their unrivalled tolerance of spice. But, as Poupe goes to bite into his poppadom, the unthinkable happens. A foul smell fills the air. Poupe knows just what this means: one of the friends has shat themselves. His evening off once again ruined by a reckless approach to spice, the Inspector must find out which gut-churning combination of curry, side dish and drink led to this mess, as well as whose pants need to be dry-cleaned.

SUSPECTS

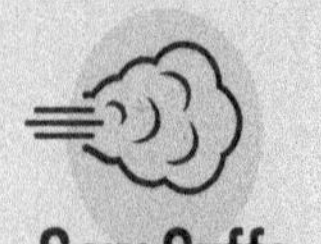

Gary Guffs

Talks the talk about his spice tolerance, but can he walk the walk (or will it be more of a waddle)?

6'1" – BADMINTON – MULLET

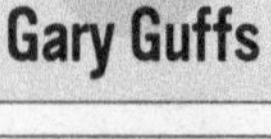

Johnny Nugs

A strapping rugby lad. He's been known to consume four naans and eleven pints in one sitting.

6'4" – RUGBY – SHAVED HEAD

Shazza Thongs

Sharon to her family, Shazza to her mates.

5'4" – FOOTBALL – BOB

Windy Wendy

You can imagine how she earned the nickname.

5'2" – DANCE – PERM

CURRY

Chicken Bhuna

A medium level of heat, but still has some people sweating.

Lamb Vindaloo

One of the hottest items on the menu; not for the faint of heart.

Prawn Madras

The risky combination of seafood and spice.

Vegetable Phaal

A red-hot rush for thrill-seekers. The Scotch bonnets will punch you in the gut.

SIDE DISH

Naan

Soaks up every last bit of sauce for maximum impact.

Onion Bhaji

Beautiful golden balls.

Pilau Rice

Sometimes the grains make it out the other end.

Samosa

Can hold a deceptive level of spice.

DRINK

Lager	Red Wine
How many pints, nobody knows. They lost count after six.	For the more sophisticated palate.

Stout	Vodka
A lot for the stomach to handle.	Not a classic accompaniment, but who cares!

CLUES

- Nobody dipped a naan in the madras.
- The chap with a mullet hoofed several pints of lager.
- Samosas and red wine could never go together. Ever.
- The rugby player was torn between the onion bhaji and the samosa.
- The dish with a medium level of heat paired perfectly with the pilau rice and vodka.
- The person that ordered the vindaloo supped a drink that revealed they had a sophisticated palate.
- The shortest of the four risked it all with the dish containing Scotch bonnet chillies.
- **The madras ended in a terrible mess.**

		DRINK				SIDE DISH				CURRY		
	Lager	Red Wine	Stout	Vodka	Naan	Onion Bhaji	Pilau Rice	Samosa	Chicken Bhuna	Lamb Vindaloo	Prawn Madras	Vegetable Phaal
SUSPECTS												
Gary Guffs												
Johnny Nugs												
Shazza Thongs												
Windy Wendy												
CURRY												
Chicken Bhuna												
Lamb Vindaloo												
Prawn Madras												
Vegetable Phaal												
SIDE DISH												
Naan												
Onion Bhaji												
Pilau Rice												
Samosa												

WHICH CURRY DID THEY EAT?

WHAT SIDE DID THEY HAVE?

WHO SOILED THEMSELVES?

WHAT DID THEY DRINK?

Suspects	Curry	Side Dish	Drink
Gary Guffs			
Johnny Nugs			
Shazza Thongs			
Windy Wendy			

15. CATS THAT CRAP

A rescue centre asks Inspector Poupe to investigate why these four cats have been returned not long after being adopted. He learns that all of them drove their owners up the wall, but only one committed the cardinal sin of crapping in the house. Poupe soon figures out which cat did the crap, which families had adopted them, what they had eaten and what other trouble they had caused.

SUSPECTS

Kitty Shat

A young pedigree with a beautiful coat. Shame about the smell.

AGE 3 – FEMALE – BLACK

Shabby Tabby

Scruffy but affectionate. She dribbles.

AGE 5 – FEMALE – TABBY

Turdles

A fierce tomcat missing a piece of his ear. He will scent-mark you.

AGE 8 – MALE – GINGER

Weelix

A mischievous moggy who's never been house-trained.

AGE 4 – MALE – BLACK AND WHITE

ADOPTIVE FAMILY

Aynous

A proud family of Norman stock. It's pronounced 'Aynes'.

Fowles

Fowles by name, foul by nature.

Gassmann

A German family who delight in sauerkraut and sprouts.

Stinker

Mr. Stinker works in sewage, as did his father, and his father before him.

CRIME

Brought In A Mouse

Why are you so mad at me? It's a gift, silly human!

Scratched The Sofa

If you won't provide a scratching-post, your finest furniture will do.

Spat Up A Hairball

By the time you hear the coughing, it's too late for your carpet.

Urinated On The Carpet

Toilets are a social concept. Cats do what they like.

FOOD

Catnip Biscuits	Dry Cat Food
2 out of 3 cats love them.	Crumbly, crunchy and easily trodden into the carpet.

Fish	Wet Cat Food
Fresh and greasy – a real treat!	This jelly-like substance looks very much the same coming out the other end.

CLUES

- The Gassmann family fed their cat the freshest fish.
- The all-black cat was fed wet cat food. That may, in hindsight, have been a mistake.
- The Stinker family were at their wits' end after their new cat hawked up a humongous hairball.
- The Fowles family adopted a tabby cat.
- The younger male cat either caught a mouse as a gift for his humans or scratched the sofa to shreds.
- The older female cat gave up hunting mice long ago.
- The damp patch that one cat created when it urinated on the carpet smelled fishy.
- Whichever feline scratched the sofa hadn't been fed the food that is easily trodden into the carpet.
- **The cat's crap was found next to a dead mouse.**

	FOOD				CRIME				ADOPTIVE FAMILY			
	Catnip Biscuits	Dry Cat Food	Fish	Wet Cat Food	Brought In A Mouse	Scratched The Sofa	Spat Up A Hairball	Urinated On The Carpet	Aynous	Fowles	Gassmann	Stinker
SUSPECTS												
Kitty Shat												
Shabby Tabby												
Turdles												
Weelix												
ADOPTIVE FAMILY												
Aynous												
Fowles												
Gassmann												
Stinker												
CRIME												
Brought In A Mouse												
Scratched The Sofa												
Spat Up A Hairball												
Urinated On The Carpet												

WHO HAD ADOPTED THEM?

WHAT OTHER CRIMES DID THEY COMMIT?

WHICH CAT DID THE CRAP?

WHAT HAD THEY EATEN?

Suspects	Adoptive Family	Crime	Food
Kitty Shat			
Shabby Tabby			
Turdles			
Weelix			

16. SHOWROOM SHITSHOW

The four Shit siblings – Doug, Jack, Noah and Gytha – have decided to buy a house together. They visit a furniture showroom, spraying themselves with rare and rancid perfumes beforehand to make the best impression. Towards the end of their visit, a sales assistant realises that one of the Shits has shat in the showroom shitter. The warehouse immediately enters lockdown, and the Shits are restrained by burly security guards until Inspector Poupe arrives. He determines who did the poo, which room they were in, what they had eaten for breakfast and the perfume they were wearing.

SUSPECTS

Doug Shit

The eldest Shit sibling, Doug is passionate about his hobbies.

5'8" – BROWN HAIR – AGE 27

Gytha Shit

The only daughter of the Shit family, she famously can't be bothered.

5'2" – GINGER HAIR – AGE 19

Jack Shit

A very knowledgeable young man, and the second of the Shit children.

6'0" – BROWN HAIR – AGE 24

Noah Shit

Gytha's twin brother. A straight talker.

5'7" – GINGER HAIR – AGE 19

LOCATION

Bathroom

Too late, the culprit realised the showroom toilets weren't plumbed.

Bedroom

You aren't allowed to jump on the beds, but did that ever stop anyone?

Kitchen

It's not a real kitchen unless the oven is dripping with grease and the sink is blocked with week-old peas.

Living Room

Where to go if you want to buy an overpriced lampshade.

BREAKFAST

Banana

About the size and shape of a large turd.

Boiled Eggs

Bodybuilders eat several of these each morning to increase their muscles, but often only succeed in increasing their flatulence.

Croissant

A curved French pastry. If inedible, may be used as a boomerang.

Yoghurt

Containing real prunes, which are known as a natural laxative.

SCENT

Civet Oil

A medieval perfume extracted from the civet, a furry mammal.

Odour de Colon

A modern perfume extracted from... best not ask.

Odour de Toilette

Because we shouldn't waste water.

Rafflesia Rapture

Harvested from a Sumatran plant said to smell like a rotten corpse. Enchanting!

CLUES

- Noah Shit ate a whole banana.
- Before arriving at the showroom, the Shit sister sprayed herself with Odour de Toilette.
- After the Shits were kicked out, the living room had to be fumigated to remove the smell of Odour de Colon.
- Doug Shit spent his time either in the bedroom or the kitchen.
- The Shit who ate the food item favoured by bodybuilders didn't enter the show kitchen.
- Whoever had a French pastry for breakfast turned up reeking of Odour de Toilette.
- Gytha's twin brother hung around the bathroom.
- Someone tried to mask the eggy farts resulting from their breakfast of choice with a spray of Rafflesia Rapture, which made them smell like a rotten corpse.
- **The show toilet is, unsurprisingly, in the show bathroom.**

		SCENT				BREAKFAST				LOCATION			
		Civet Oil	Odour de Colon	Odour de Toilette	Rafflesia Rapture	Banana	Boiled Eggs	Croissant	Yoghurt	Bathroom	Bedroom	Kitchen	Living Room
SUSPECTS	Doug Shit												
	Gytha Shit												
	Jack Shit												
	Noah Shit												
LOCATION	Bathroom												
	Bedroom												
	Kitchen												
	Living Room												
BREAKFAST	Banana												
	Boiled Eggs												
	Croissant												
	Yoghurt												

WHERE DID THEY DO IT?

WHAT HAD THEY EATEN?

WHO DID THE POO?

WHAT PERFUME HAD THEY APPLIED?

Suspects	Location	Breakfast	Scent
Doug Shit			
Gytha Shit			
Jack Shit			
Noah Shit			

17. SCHOOL STOOLS

Inspector Poupe is called to St. Crapola's Grammar School to investigate the appearance of a suspicious turd on the school property. His gut tells him that one of the teachers was behind this (and if there's one thing Poupe trusts, it's his gut). After some digging, he finds out what subject is taught by each member of staff, where they were at lunchtime and what they ate. By putting these pieces together, he will soon find the culprit.

SUSPECTS

Miss Privy

Mild-mannered and gentle. Will let students take the piss, or take a piss, at their leisure.

5'3" – BLONDE HAIR – BROWN EYES

Mr. Head

Popular with the kids. Loves a bit of banter and always turns up in a novelty tie.

6'0" – GINGER HAIR – GREEN EYES

Mr. Lav

One of the strictest, most feared teachers in the school. He won't even allow bathroom breaks.

5'8" – GREY HAIR – BLUE EYES

Mrs. Crapper

Her heart is in the right place, but is her poo?

5'5" – BROWN HAIR – HAZEL EYES

LOCATION

Canteen

Hard to tell if the smell is the food or something else.

Classroom

Rows of desks covered in chewing gum.

Hall

Echoing and cavernous with a lingering scent of BO.

Sports Field

Might there be something else for the hurdlers to jump over?

SUBJECT

French

Caca! Merde! Crottes!

Geography

Can help you locate the toilets.

Maths

Will teach you all about number ones and number twos.

Music

Humming a scale mid-dump can help disguise any telltale sounds.

Baked Potato	Caesar Salad
The inside is the hottest substance known to man.	Supposedly 'healthy' but really just a pile of croutons and cheese.

Ham Sandwich	Instant Noodles
With white bread so flimsy it dissolves upon eye contact.	Unapologetically delicious junk food.

CLUES

- The brown-haired teacher had flimsy white bread for lunch.
- One teacher went for a run around the sports field. They tried to kid themselves that their Caesar salad was also a healthy choice.
- The teacher with hazel eyes is either the maths teacher or the music teacher.
- Mr. Lav had tuna on his baked potato.
- The music teacher did not have a ham sandwich or noodles.
- The tallest teacher spent lunch leading tiddlywinks club in a location that had an unpleasant smell of BO.
- The French teacher stood in the canteen wrinkling their nose at most of the food on offer.
- **The poo was found under a desk.**

		LUNCH				SUBJECT				LOCATION			
		Baked Potato	Caesar Salad	Ham Sandwich	Instant Noodles	French	Geography	Maths	Music	Canteen	Classroom	Hall	Sports Field
SUSPECTS	Miss Privy												
	Mr. Head												
	Mr. Lav												
	Mrs. Crapper												
LOCATION	Canteen												
	Classroom												
	Hall												
	Sports Field												
SUBJECT	French												
	Geography												
	Maths												
	Music												

WHERE DID THEY POO?

WHAT DO THEY TEACH?

WHO DID THE POO?

WHAT DID THEY HAVE FOR LUNCH?

Suspects	Location	Subject	Lunch
Miss Privy			
Mr. Head			
Mr. Lav			
Mrs. Crapper			

18. ROYAL FLUSH

Inspector Poupe is called to a ball at Arseware Palace, an event attended by all the senior royals! However, much to his disappointment, he is not there as a guest. Poupe has a case to solve. Somebody has forgotten to flush, leaving the fine Arseware porcelain smeared with distinctly royal faeces. Poupe records the shape and colour of the stool, then works out the name and title of the royal offender.

SUSPECTS

Augufftus

A jolly fellow who partakes in much hearty belly-laughing and backslapping.

GREEN EYES – BEARD – TERRIER

Beedlebum

Likes a drink or two... or fifteen.

BROWN EYES – BOW TIE – PARROT

Pottyson

Does his 'duty' with grace and decorum.

BLUE EYES – GLASSES – SIAMESE CAT

Thomass

Notoriously eccentric, he is known for keeping exotic pets and chatting with them often.

HAZEL EYES – TOP HAT – OSTRICH

TITLE

Duke

Duke of Shitterton, to be precise.

Earl

Developing his own brand of tea, with notes of tarmac and tobacco.

King

Looks majestic sat on the throne.

Prince

A prince among men, indeed.

STOOL COLOUR

Chocolate

An appealing shade of brown, almost good enough to eat!

Dark Brown

A disconcerting shade verging on black.

Golden

A stool fit for a king! Or any nobleman for that matter.

Yellow

Formed from a diet of English mustard and piccalilli.

STOOL SHAPE

Liquefied	Long and Smooth
A nightmare for the housekeeping staff to clean.	A gloriously healthy specimen. Slides out a dream.

Lumpy	Round
Painfully squeezed from the intestine.	Like small, dainty rabbit pellets.

CLUES

- One royal filled the bowl with yellow liquid, but at least they did so with grace and decorum.
- The terrier barked as his master produced a chocolatey turd.
- Duke Beedlebum of Shitterton spent the ball getting positively shit-faced.
- Augufftus could be a prince or a king.
- The prince's stools are not long and smooth.
- The glamour of the golden stool was lessened by its lumpiness.
- The earl produces perfectly spherical droppings.
- **The perfect stool – long and smooth – was found floating in the toilet.**

		STOOL SHAPE				STOOL COLOUR				TITLE			
		Liquefied	Long and Smooth	Lumpy	Round	Chocolate	Dark Brown	Golden	Yellow	Duke	Earl	King	Prince
SUSPECTS	Augufftus												
	Beedlebum												
	Pottyson												
	Thomass												
TITLE	Duke												
	Earl												
	King												
	Prince												
STOOL COLOUR	Chocolate												
	Dark Brown												
	Golden												
	Yellow												

WHAT WAS THEIR TITLE?

WHAT COLOUR WAS THEIR POO?

WHO DIDN'T FLUSH?

WHAT WAS THE SHAPE OF THEIR POO?

Suspects	Title	Stool Colour	Stool Shape
Augufftus			
Beedlebum			
Pottyson			
Thomass			

19. LOVE AT FIRST SHITE

Welcome to *Love At First Shite*, the dating show where female contestants pick partners based purely on their poo! Don't tell anyone, but this show is Inspector Poupe's guilty pleasure. On this week's episode, one lucky lady met her husband-to-be! Unfortunately she was so excited when she met her match that she pooed herself in the dressing room afterwards. Poupe has no problem working out the culprit by deducing each contestant's occupation, poo preference and their match.

SUSPECTS

Janey Crack

An easy-going gal looking for someone she can fart in front of.

5'6" – BRUNETTE – SCOUSE

Kim Smellsbum

Just wants someone to make her poo herself laughing.

5'4" – GINGER – COCKNEY

Lucy Loo

Loves cooking, long walks and outdoor poos.

5'7" – BLEACH BLONDE – GEORDIE

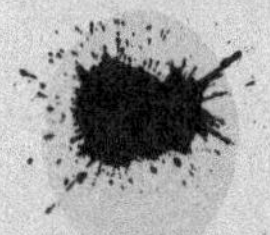

Sue Idge

Thirty, flirty and shingles.

5'5" – DIRTY BLONDE – MANCUNIAN

OCCUPATION

Gastroenterologist

An expert in all things bowel-related.

Plumber

A master of the dating game, always willing to take the plunge.

Sewage Worker

Luckily the smell of poo comes out in the shower.

Toilet Cleaner

Takes great pride in keeping the porcelain sparkling.

POO PREFERENCE

Curly

Reminiscent of soft serve ice cream.

Dark

Tall, dark and handsome, as the saying goes.

Shiny

A smooth, glistening surface that glides through the colon.

Speckled

The specks of vegetables tell a story.

MATCH

Bobby Floater Tatted stud on the outside, big softie on the inside.	**Keith Downunder** An upbeat Australian with a lust for life.
Paul Potty Enjoys football, football and football.	**Tommy Twos** A chartered accountant whose idea of quirkiness is wearing odd socks.

CLUES

- The ginger-haired contestant turned her nose up at the Australian's stool: she could never be paired with him!
- The Mancunian was drawn to either Keith Downunder or Paul Potty based on their poos.
- The tatted stud does lovely shiny poos.
- Tommy Twos matched with the master of the dating game.
- The easy-going gal did not like Bobby Floater's poo, so he couldn't be her match.
- The sewage worker goes crazy for dark poos.
- The shortest contestant is a toilet cleaner who loves a crap that reminds her of ice cream.
- **The bride-to-be is a professional gastroenterologist.**

		MATCH				POO PREFERENCE				OCCUPATION			
		Bobby Floater	Keith Downunder	Paul Potty	Tommy Twos	Curly	Dark	Shiny	Speckled	Gastroenterologist	Plumber	Sewage Worker	Toilet Cleaner
SUSPECTS	Janey Crack												
	Kim Smellsbum												
	Lucy Loo												
	Sue Idge												
OCCUPATION	Gastroenterologist												
	Plumber												
	Sewage Worker												
	Toilet Cleaner												
POO PREFERENCE	Curly												
	Dark												
	Shiny												
	Speckled												

WHAT IS THEIR OCCUPATION?

WHAT TYPE OF POO DO THEY LIKE?

WHO MET THEIR FUTURE HUSBAND?

WHO DID THEY MATCH WITH?

Suspects	Occupation	Poo Preference	Match
Janey Crack			
Kim Smellsbum			
Lucy Loo			
Sue Idge			

20. BOTTOM BURPS

Arty Farty had a party to celebrate the birthday of his friend, Ivana Dump. What better party entertainment could there be than a farting game called Bottom Burps: whoever farts for the longest time, wins. Stopwatches at the ready! Unfortunately one of the four competition participants broke the cardinal rule of a farting game and followed through, doing a mini poo in their pants. Not cool. All four denied committing the whoopsie and so it was left to Inspector Poupe to examine the evidence and reveal who should be banned from any future farting competitions. He soon worked out whose fart became a shart, how long it lasted, how loud it was and what it smelt of.

SUSPECTS

Arty Farty

Farty by name and by nature, this young man sure loves to trump.

5'8" – HAZEL EYES – AGE 19

Guffy Buffy

Has a constant case of verbal diarrhoea, but was she the one to follow through?

5'6" – GREEN EYES – AGE 20

Ivana Dump

This girl always has two poos a day, even when she doesn't need them.

5'5" – HAZEL EYES – AGE 18

Smelly Kelly

Given her nickname by her flatmates as she eats asparagus daily, as attested to by her smelly wee.

5'4" – BROWN EYES – AGE 21

FART DURATION (SECONDS)

3.14

Also known as a 'pi' fart, for obvious reasons.

5

The five-second rule is supposed to be about dropping food on the floor, not dropping a fart, but never mind.

9.7

The world's best can run 100 metres in the time this fart took to finish.

11.2

This description isn't long-winded. An 11.2 second fart is very long-winded.

LOUDNESS

10 decibels

This fart didn't trouble the eardrums, making about as much noise as breathing in or out.

40 decibels

Perceptible to the ear, but just barely. This fart was about as loud as talking quietly.

80 decibels

Now we're talking. A beauty this loud would wake you up from even a sound slumber.

90 decibels

This wouldn't quite register as an earthquake, but it's still very loud – about as noisy as a passing tube train!

BOUQUET

Mouldy Cheese	Rotten Eggs
Complete with overtones of bitter cheddar. Enjoy!	Your common-or-garden fart scent. Gas masks at the ready!

Sour Milk	Stinky Tofu
The whiff from this fart will spoil even the freshest of milk.	Even the hardened farter will be pleading for a peg for their nose after smelling this bad boy.

CLUES

- The fart whose length is also known as a 'pi' wasn't as loud as a tube train.
- The longest-lasting fart smelt like mouldy cheese and registered at the 40 decibels mark.
- The asparagus-lover did the quietest fart, but perhaps the smell made up for it.
- The five-second fart did not lead to partygoers pleading for nose pegs.
- The producer of the loudest fart created a distinctively unpleasant eggy fug.
- The girl who always has two poos a day produced either the 3.14 second fart or the 9.7 second fart.
- The 19-year-old host of the party made his mark on the Bottom Burps competition by producing a little ripper that smelt of stinky tofu.
- **The person who followed through produced a milky-smelling fart.**

		BOUQUET				LOUDNESS				FART DURATION		
	Mouldy Cheese	Rotten Eggs	Sour Milk	Stinky Tofu	10 decibels	40 decibels	80 decibels	90 decibels	3.14	5	9.7	11.2
SUSPECTS: Arty Farty												
Guffy Buffy												
Ivana Dump												
Smelly Kelly												
FART DURATION: 3.14 secs												
5 secs												
9.7 secs												
11.2 secs												
LOUDNESS: 10 decibels												
40 decibels												
80 decibels												
90 decibels												

HOW LONG DID THEIR FART LAST?

HOW LOUD WAS IT?

WHO FOLLOWED THROUGH?

WHAT DID IT SMELL OF?

Suspects	Fart Duration	Loudness	Bouquet
Arty Farty			
Guffy Buffy			
Ivana Dump			
Smelly Kelly			

CONSTIPATION: HARD

EXHIBIT C

When tackling hard cases, Inspector Poupe swears by his bullshit detector for help.

He picked it up at a bargain price online and, inexplicably, it has a habit of providing him with a clue when he most needs it.

The only downside is the only instructions it came with were pretty incoherent – something about "white = bowel, grey = incontinent". Something got lost in translation, perhaps.

You'll need to work out the letter of the alphabet assigned to each symbol to help you use the bullshit detector successfully.

1 = ___ 1 = ___ 8 = ___ 15 = ___

2 = ___ 2 = ___ 9 = ___ 16 = ___

3 = ___ 3 = ___ 10 = ___ 17 = ___

4 = ___ 4 = ___ 11 = ___ 18 = ___

5 = ___ 5 = ___ 12 = ___ 19 = ___

6 = ___ 13 = ___ 20 = ___

7 = ___ 14 = ___ 21 = ___

1. POOP DECK

The poop deck is the highest deck of a ship. During his morning inspection of the boat, the Captain of the *Sin King* has to his horror found a literal poop on the poop deck. Trying not to keel over from the stench of the turd, he summons the crew. He needs to find out who did it so he can continue to run a tight ship. All deny knowledge, but four of them seem particularly fidgety and he believes one of them is the culprit. As luck would have it, Inspector Poupe is on board enjoying a cruise. The Captain likes the cut of his jib and tasks him with working out who did the poop based on their job, years at sea and possible motive.

SUSPECTS

Ann Kerr

Ann suffered from terrible seasickness as a child, so a career working on boats seemed only logical. The initial results were messy.

5'4" – BLONDE HAIR – BROWN EYES

Ash Orr

Ash is the biggest joker among all the crew, so is likely to find the idea of a poop on the poop deck almost irresistible. But that doesn't mean he definitely did it...

5'7" – BLACK HAIR – HAZEL EYES

Cat A. Meringue

Cat never particularly wanted to work on a boat, but when her partner got a job on a cruise ship she decided to join him to test the water. That relation-ship is now over.

5'9" – BLONDE HAIR – GREEN EYES

Dec Hand

Dec decided he wanted to go to sea after he watched a documentary all about ships and shipbuilding. He found it truly oar-some.

5'11" – BROWN HAIR – BLUE EYES

JOB TITLE

Chef

Chef's favourite drink?
A nice bottle of port, of course.
But was he sober today?

Croupier

Entertainment is very important when you are stuck on a steel vessel bobbing up and down on the water for weeks at a time. Without it, you might keel over from boredom.

Disc Jockey

This disc jockey is legendary for the cheesiness of the music that they play. It proves wildly popular with the punters however, and at the end of each set they take a bow.

Security Officer

As a security officer it's very important to project the right image and take everything seriously to reassure the cruisers. There's no time for frivolity – you have to be very stern.

YEARS AT SEA

1

Basically still a landlubber, nothing is plain sailing.

2

After two years on the briny, you're worth your salt.

3

Three years seems like a long time to be at sea. But whatever floats your boat.

4

After this many years at sea, everything looks shipshape.

POSSIBLE MOTIVE

Dare	Dislike Captain
Doing a poo just for a dare? You're sailing close to the wind.	If this is your reason for a cheeky poop-deck poop, your career could be dead in the water.

Drunk	Pay Dispute
If you're three sheets to the wind, maybe it would have seemed a good idea to do a poo.	If you're not on board with your remuneration you might decide to make waves.

CLUES

- With the boat being rocked by a strong wave, someone hands Poupe a note that reads "EHTYTCIESRU IRFEOFC IS PNPUYHA ITWH TIEHR APY".
- The shortest of the four suspects has been at sea for two years longer than the person who was potentially motivated by drink.
- The person with black hair has not been at sea for two years.
- The chef has been out on the waves for more time than the person whose career would be dead in the water if they were found guilty.
- The person who used to suffer from seasickness thinks they should be paid more money.
- The person who plays cheesy music has been at sea for two years longer than Dec Hand.
- **The mystery pooper did it for a dare.**

		POSSIBLE MOTIVE				YEARS AT SEA				JOB TITLE			
		Dare	Dislike Captain	Drunk	Pay Dispute	1	2	3	4	Chef	Croupier	Disc Jockey	Security Officer
SUSPECTS	Ann Kerr												
	Ash Orr												
	Cat A. Meringue												
	Dec Hand												
JOB TITLE	Chef												
	Croupier												
	Disc Jockey												
	Security Officer												
YEARS AT SEA	1												
	2												
	3												
	4												

WHAT'S THEIR JOB ON BOARD?

HOW MANY YEARS HAVE THEY BEEN AT SEA?

WHO DID THE POO?

WHAT WAS THEIR MOTIVE?

Suspects	Job title	Years at sea	Possible motive
Ann Kerr			
Ash Orr			
Cat A. Meringue			
Dec Hand			

2. DONKEY PONG

Members of the public have decamped to the beach one sunny Sunday. An idyllic scene ensues of people having fun in the sun, splashing in the sea, donkeys giving giggling children a ride and... a poo on the sand! Despite the beachgoers all trying to pin the blame for the poo on one of the donkeys, the authorities are confident the crap is human, and have narrowed the search for the culprit down to these four families. To finish the job, Poupe is called in to work out where each group of suspects were on the beach, the size of their party (not including their pet pooch: dogs are supposedly banned on this beach, after all) and the colour of their windbreak. He'll soon find out which family the offender belongs to.

SUSPECTS

The Bottoms

You can bet your bottom dollar that you'll find this perma-tanned family at the beach catching some rays.

ARRIVED AT 1PM – LABRADOR – LIVE NEARBY

The Dumps

This family once forgot to put the bins out and, ever since, have been known by the neighbours as the Rubbish Dumps.

ARRIVED AT 3PM – POODLE – ON HOLIDAY

The Parps

Mr. Parp is something of an aggressive driver and is always beeping his horn at other drivers, so the family name is rather apt.

ARRIVED AT 2PM – SPANIEL – DAY TRIP

The Windies

No, no, you're mispronouncing it! It's not 'wind' as in farting, it's 'wind' as in twist and turn.

ARRIVED AT 4PM – GOLDEN RETRIEVER – ON HOLIDAY

BEACH LOCATION

Damp Sand

One family set up camp on the darker sand revealed by the ebbing tide. Guaranteed to result in soggy bottoms.

Dry Sand

The sensible choice, equidistant between the sea for number ones, and when nature truly comes a-calling, the café toilets for number twos.

Rock Pool

Perfect for those who like catching crabs.

Sand Dunes

Sheltering behind the sand dunes reassures you that there is at least one type of wind you can protect yourself from.

PARTY SIZE

2

Would it be poetic justice if the group of two produced the number two?

3

Three's a crowd, particularly if one of that crowd produces an illicit poo.

4

A group of four adults: that's four mouths... and four bottoms.

5

Give me five! But no poo, please.

WINDBREAK COLOUR

Brown

A shade somewhere between coffee and chocolate reminiscent of... don't go there.

Green

The colour of grass. And poo, apparently, if you've eaten enough spinach.

Orange

Easily located on the beach after a dip in the sea, the perfect choice for one family of myopic beachgoers.

Sand

What better colour could there be for a windbreak on the beach than a perfectly camouflaged sandy shade?

CLUES

- The group of four adults had a bright green windbreak.
- The family who arrived at 3pm had one more member in their party than the family who sat on dry sand.
- The family who sited themselves at a location that is perfect for catching crabs had a brown windbreak.
- Someone with verbal diarrhoea told Poupe the following:

  "THE MTOSBTO DDI NTO TSI ON PDMA ASDN".
- The family who were accompanied by their poodle consisted of one person less than the family who had an orange windbreak.
- The family who live nearby had two more members in their party than the family enjoying a day trip.
- **The poo was, fittingly, found by the brown windbreak.**

		WINDBREAK COLOUR				PARTY SIZE				BEACH LOCATION			
		Brown	Green	Orange	Sand	2	3	4	5	Damp Sand	Dry Sand	Rock Pool	Sand Dunes
SUSPECTS	The Bottoms												
	The Dumps												
	The Parps												
	The Windies												
BEACH LOCATION	Damp Sand												
	Dry Sand												
	Rock Pool												
	Sand Dunes												
PARTY SIZE	2												
	3												
	4												
	5												

WHERE ON THE BEACH WERE THEY LOCATED?

HOW MANY FAMILY MEMBERS WERE ON THE BEACH?

WHICH FAMILY DID THE BEACH CRAPPER BELONG TO?

WHAT COLOUR WINDBREAK DID THE FAMILY HAVE?

Suspects	Beach Location	Party Size	Windbreak Colour
The Bottoms			
The Dumps			
The Parps			
The Windies			

3. ACROSS THE POONIVERSE

In space, no one can hear you poo. When an enormous turd floating through Quadrant 12 Beta fatally collides with a shuttle, Inspector Poupe watches on from his spaceship in horror. This was not what he had planned when booking a relaxing space cruise. However, it is now up to him to track down the alien culprit, their planet of origin, their distance from home and their disastrous diet.

SUSPECTS

Assoroth

A bad-tempered, tentacled tyrant, responsible for the staining of many a pair of spacepants.

PURPLE – COMMANDER – SUCKERS

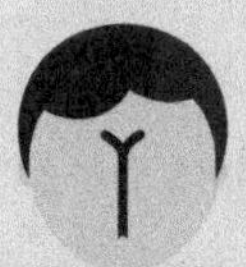

Bumrox

With a face that looks like a bottom and a bottom like a face.

RED – PILOT – ANTENNAE

Lax'tiv

A member of the Quik'lax race. Their skin secretes a substance with magical laxative powers.

GREEN – DOCTOR – SLIMY

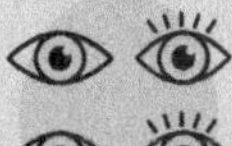

Poozorg

Leader of the Pooman Race – one of the few species in the universe to defecate through their earholes.

BLUE – PRESIDENT – 200 EYES

PLANET

Alpha Latrina

The inhabitants of this world worship manure for its fertilising, life-giving properties. Whole temples have been constructed in its honour.

Fartacus Minor

If you think it smells bad here, you should try visiting Fartacus Major.

Krapton

Home to a powerful alien race with radioactive faeces.

Poopiter

A huge gas giant with great lakes of explosive methane – what could possibly go wrong?

DISTANCE TRAVELLED

100 light years

A quick hop, you would think, but a jam on the intergalactic highway really dragged the journey out.

150 light years

Stick on a podcast, listen to some music, and the journey will fly by.

200 light years

Before embarking on a journey of this length, a precautionary toilet trip is essential.

250 light years

Luckily, they took a short cut through the Portaloo Wormhole.

FOOD

Bin Juice

Made from the ripest bin fruits, a speciality of the Bilgeway galaxy.

Moon Cheese

Mined from the moons of Stinkorius Delta, its distinctive odour of sweaty socks is admired across the pooniverse.

Space Beans

Produces farts that will blast you into space.

Splatterfruit

A sumptuous brown fruit which falls and splatters when ripe.

CLUES

- The pilot has travelled 200 light years.
- Lax'tiv was glad not to be sharing a ship with the space bean eater who had 100 light years longer in which to fill their cabin with gas.
- The tentacled extraterrestrial downed a huge vat of bin juice. Delish!
- Poupe's spaceship received a coded distress signal. It read: "EHT ERD AENIL AHD TON EBEN AINTGE CESAP SAENB".
- Ding! Ding! Just then Poupe's bullshit detector came to life and showed the following code:

  [See Exhibit C]

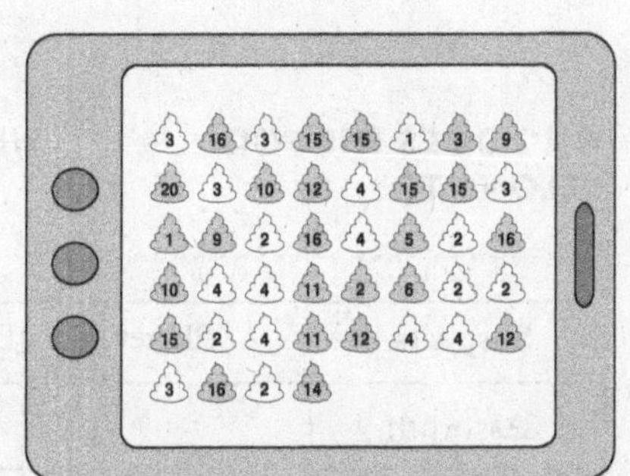

- Krapton is 50 light years closer to Quadrant 12 Beta than the home planet of the alien that ate splatterfruit.
- Assoroth has travelled 50 light years less distance than the manure-worshipper.
- **Analysis concluded the turd must have come from an inhabitant of Fartacus Minor.**

		FOOD				DISTANCE TRAVELLED				PLANET			
		Bin Juice	Moon Cheese	Space Beans	Splatterfruit	100 light years	150 light years	200 light years	250 light years	Alpha Latrina	Fartacus Minor	Krapton	Poopiter
SUSPECTS	Assoroth												
	Bumrox												
	Lax'tiv												
	Poozorg												
PLANET	Alpha Latrina												
	Fartacus Minor												
	Krapton												
	Poopiter												
DISTANCE TRAVELLED	100 light years												
	150 light years												
	200 light years												
	250 light years												

WHAT IS THEIR HOME PLANET?

HOW FAR HAVE THEY TRAVELLED?

WHO DOES THE POO BELONG TO?

WHAT DO THEY EAT?

Suspects	Planet	Distance Travelled	Food
Assoroth			
Bumrox			
Lax'tiv			
Poozorg			

4. PRIVY COUNCIL

There's controversy in Looville. Four local councillors have all wanted to take credit for the installation of new public toilet facilities by the beach. All four turned up to the opening ceremony and, once the mayor cut the tape, were the first to use the facilities. Each councillor gave a different toilet a test run. Unfortunately one has committed a little faux pas and done a poo on the toilet seat. The mayor can't get to the bottom of it, as the politicians are experts of getting themselves out of any hole. Exasperated, he calls for Poupe who has been spotted sunbathing on the beach. He soon works out which toilet each councillor used, their party colours and slogan, and makes short work of deducing whose career is about to go down the toilet.

SUSPECTS

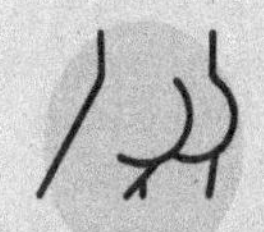

Ben Down

An experienced councillor, Ben has won a lot of votes over the years purely due to his name and the puerile sense of humour of many of his constituents. Most of his policies are crap.

6'1" – BROWN EYES – BROWN HAIR

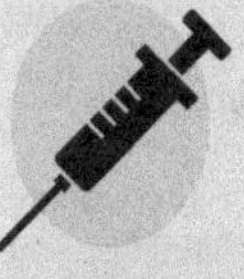

Enni Ma

Ever since getting caught short one unforgettable Sunday, Enni has championed increasing the number of publicly accessible facilities. Now that constituents with smartphones are everywhere, she simply can't risk having another little accident.

5'6" – BLUE EYES – BLONDE HAIR

Jimmy Riddle

Jimmy fancies himself as something of a wheeler-dealer, a man who can get things done. Unfortunately he's full of hot air. And quite a bit of crap, judging by the council toilets.

5'10" – BLUE EYES – BROWN HAIR

Mayka Puddle

Mayka has an unusual name, but then her parents have a very unusual sense of humour. She wants to make sure that accidental puddles when out and about are a thing of the past.

5'8" – HAZEL EYES – GREY HAIR

TOILET USED

One

A little bit of luxury away from home! A lot of the budget for the new facilities was blown on toilet one, which is twice the size of the others and comes with one of those fancy air fresheners that sprays automatically when it detects motion. Bliss.

Two

Toilet number two is always going to be the traditionalist's toilet of choice for doing a number two when out and about. As such the toilet brush in this one will see a lot of active duty.

Three

A bit like a terraced house, toilet number three leaves something to be desired: you'll hear unpleasant sounds coming from both sides when the neighbouring toilets are occupied, and that's not something you'd wish on your worst enemy.

Four

The toilet connoisseur's toilet of choice. It's at the end, so there's not going to be anyone walking past you, and as it's further away than the others most people won't bother walking to the end. If you want to poo in relative peace, toilet four's your best choice.

PARTY COLOURS

Beige

When the party set up its headquarters the building contained a very tasteful beige-coloured toilet. It seemed only right and proper to adopt that shade as the party's official colour.

Black and White

A black and white issue seems simple and obvious. Likewise, the party with black and white colours believes that voting for them should be a simple choice for their electorate. Unfortunately many see it as obvious that they should *not* vote for them, but them's the breaks.

Brown

The party was set up by the Brown family. That's the only reason the party rosettes are a shade of brown – despite the mud-slinging suggestions from some other parties.

Yellow

Gold brings to mind opulence, riches and even a splash of luxury. The candidate wearing yellow is more known for making a splash in a different kind of way.

Flush with Success

After getting bogged down trying to come up with something pithy, this was the best one councillor could come up with.

Free Bogroll for All

Does what it says on the tin, but whoever came up with this is hardly on a roll.

More PCs More WCs

In fairness, as party slogans go, this does everything you want: it's clear, succinct and it rhymes. Perfection in four short words.

Spend a Penny for Free

One councillor thought they were very clever for combining the literal and metaphorical senses of spending a penny in one bon mot, but will their electorate appreciate it?

CLUES

- The councillor who used the traditionalist's toilet of choice didn't campaign under the slogan 'free bogroll for all'.
- The person whose slogan is 'flush with success' used a toilet whose number is two higher than Mayka Puddle's toilet of choice.
- The party member wearing a beige rosette had a number one in toilet one. But did they also have a number two?
- The councillor with a slogan that is 'perfection' used a higher-numbered toilet than the person wearing a yellow rosette.
- The tallest councillor likes his 'flush with success' slogan.
- One eyewitness opined that, on reflection, "EHT ROLLICNUOC ROF EHT YTRAP TES PU YB EHT NWORB YLIMAF DESU A TELIOT TAHT SAW ENO REWOL NI REBMUN NAHT TAHT DESU YB INNE AM".
- **The toilet seat pooper wanted free bogroll for all.**

	ELECTION SLOGAN: Flush with Success	Free Bogroll for All	More PCs More WCs	Spend a Penny for Free	PARTY COLOURS: Beige	Black and White	Brown	Yellow	TOILET USED: One	Two	Three	Four
SUSPECTS: Ben Down												
Enni Ma												
Jimmy Riddle												
Mayka Puddle												
TOILET USED: One												
Two												
Three												
Four												
PARTY COLOURS: Beige												
Black and White												
Brown												
Yellow												

WHICH TOILET DID THEY USE?

WHAT ARE THEIR PARTY COLOURS?

WHO DID THE POO?

WHAT IS THEIR ELECTION SLOGAN?

Suspects	Toilet used	Party Colours	Election Slogan
Ben Down			
Enni Ma			
Jimmy Riddle			
Mayka Puddle			

5. POO ON THE PLANE

Poupe takes a flight with TurdLines, the only airline to have always used 100% organic fuel. Halfway through the journey, a foul stench begins to spread through the plane, starting at the toilets. It seems that one of the passengers has done a poo so foul that, even in the vacuum-packed septic tank, there's a risk of it gassing everyone onboard. Poupe is asked to investigate. After collecting information on each passenger's travel class, number of flights, and food or drink onboard, he figures out who stank out the plane.

SUSPECTS

The stress of organising a family holiday has Hannah fit to burst. If her kids start one more argument...

AGE 42 – AISLE SEAT – TRAVELLING WITH FAMILY

Letrip's teacher is seriously regretting allowing him on the trip. Whether or not he did the poo, he's a major contributor to the noxious atmosphere of this plane.

AGE 16 – MIDDLE SEAT – TRAVELLING WITH SCHOOL

For some reason, nobody ever sits next to Robin on buses, trains or planes. Even her partner insists on putting a seat between them.

AGE 33 – WINDOW SEAT – TRAVELLING WITH PARTNER

Ted got his nickname before ever setting foot on a plane. It refers to his habit of temporarily levitating when pushing out a gigantic fart.

AGE 56 – MIDDLE SEAT – TRAVELLING ALONE

TRAVEL CLASS

Business

Despite the name, these seats aren't reserved for commercial travellers. Anyone who can pay the piper can get one of these luxurious places, inferior only to first class.

Economy

Your bog-standard aeroplane seat – and I do mean bog.

First

The lushest of the lush, no longer available on many aeroplanes. First class travellers get unlimited drinks, a recliner chair and their own widescreen TV. However, that doesn't mean they can stink out the aircraft with impunity.

Premium Economy

For when you don't want to say you flew economy, but you can't afford business.

FLIGHTS TAKEN

1

This passenger is taking off for the very first time. Did pre-flight nerves loosen their bowels?

6

The novelty hasn't quite worn off for this passenger. They still stare out of the window on takeoff and hold their breath during landing.

11

Flying is more or less conventional for this passenger, although they might still get excited by heavy turbulence.

16

This passenger is a veteran of the air. They were probably a bird in a previous life, if you believe in reincarnation.

Bottled Water	**Fish**
This passenger refused to pay aeroplane prices and instead brought along their own bottle of water. By the time the plane touches down, they're chewing their nails with hunger.	Doesn't smell especially fresh, but then it is served in plastic wrapping. What's the worst that could happen?
Meat	**Porridge**
Beef, chicken or pork in tiny plastic portions.	The only veggie meal served on this plane, it's criminally overpriced.

CLUES

- Whoever ate the porridge has been on five more flights than the person travelling with their family.
- Shortly before turning his phone onto aeroplane mode, Poupe received a cryptic message that reads: "YTE'HER ESGVIRN SFHI NI SNSSBIUE SSALC".
- The passenger living it large in first class wasn't feeling like meat today.
- The business-class passenger has been on five more flights than the person in economy.
- The passenger with the window seat has been on 10 more flights than the miser who brought their own bottled water.
- The oldest suspect didn't bring their own water.
- The passenger in business class is on their sixth flight.
- **The fish caused uncontrollable flatulence, resulting in compulsive defecation.**

		AEROPLANE FOOD				FLIGHTS TAKEN				TRAVEL CLASS			
		Bottled Water	Fish	Meat	Porridge	1	6	11	16	Business	Economy	First	Premium Economy
SUSPECTS	Hannah Hugecrap												
	Liam Letrip												
	Robin Ripesmell												
	Ted Takeoff												
TRAVEL CLASS	Business												
	Economy												
	First												
	Premium Economy												
FLIGHTS TAKEN	1												
	6												
	11												
	16												

WHAT WAS THEIR TRAVEL CLASS?

HOW MANY FLIGHTS HAVE THEY BEEN ON?

WHO DID THE POO?

WHAT DID THEY EAT/DRINK ON THE AEROPLANE?

Suspects	Travel Class	Flights Taken	Aeroplane Food
Hannah Hugecrap			
Liam Letrip			
Robin Ripesmell			
Ted Takeoff			

6. FERMENTED FAECES

If you have money to spare, there's no better way to waste it than on wine-tasting. Three wealthy guests, Rebecca Reeks, Winifred Willfart and Bert Breakwind, accompanied the experienced Sommelier Stool on a tour of the cellars. Towards the close of the evening, a cluster of turds shaped almost like a bunch of grapes was found (read: trodden on) by one of the waiters. The horrified organisers call Inspector Poupe, who arrives minutes later. By sheer chance, he'd been having a tour of the vineyard. He works out who did the poo, the type and vintage of the wine they had been drinking and how intoxicated they were.

SUSPECTS

A wealthy Englishman spending his retirement sampling the best wines. He expresses his admiration for a fine vintage with a thunderclap of wind.

6'1" – STRIPED SUIT – ENGLISH

No one wants to drink from the bottle after Mrs. Reeks, so she gets it all to herself. It's probably the smell.

5'4" – RED DRESS – AMERICAN

In his capacity as a sommelier, or 'wine waiter', Monsieur Stool has helped thousands of people choose the right vintage. Just don't ask for one of his samples.

6'3" – BLACK SUIT – FRENCH

An oenophile extraordinaire, Winifred's wine-tasting adventures have taken her to all four corners of the globe despite her allergy to grapes. She can't drink a single glass without flatulence.

5'6" – BLUE DRESS – ENGLISH

VINTAGE

1945

An eye-wateringly expensive vintage bottled just after the end of the Second World War. You're paying for the history as much as the flavour: until it's uncorked, there's no way to tell if this wine will taste like honey or vinegar.

1970

Old but just about affordable if you splash out. Did the person who drank it also 'splash out' on the floor?

1995

A wine produced near the end of the millennium. It's now old enough to drink, in both senses.

2020

Cheap modern wine: does it have a laxative effect?

WINE TYPE

Assti Spufarte

A foamy beverage which some say tastes like cat's farts. How do they know that, anyway?

Chartdonhay

A French wine that tastes like hay and piss. It's pronounced 'shart'.

Pinot Marron

Lovingly made with brown grapes.

Smellion

Because the body of the wine is clear, the dark flecks are more obvious.

STATUS

Pissed	Shitfaced
Poupe doesn't investigate urine, so whether this drunk also wet themselves is irrelevant.	The opposite of 'bottoms up' is 'face down'. Let's hope this adjective is metaphorical.

Sober	Tipsy
Stone-cold sober. Did they take advantage of the others' drunkenness to drop a tacit log?	For this drinker, the party is only just getting started.

CLUES

- Neither of the women drank the 1945 wine.
- The wine that tastes like cat's farts was produced 50 years after the Chartdonhay.
- The drinker for whom the party was only getting started sampled a wine that was made 50 years after the Smellion.
- The sommelier helped himself to a wine from 1995. The wine the 'pissed' guest drank had been made 25 years earlier.
- One of the drunks muttered something under their breath. To Poupe, it sounded like "HET RIAEMNAC DEYSAT SBERO".
- **The shitter was truly shitfaced.**

		STATUS				WINE TYPE				VINTAGE			
		Pissed	Shitfaced	Sober	Tipsy	Assti Spufarte	Chartdonhay	Pinot Marron	Smellion	1945	1970	1995	2020
SUSPECTS	Bert Breakwind												
	Rebecca Reeks												
	Sommelier Stool												
	Winifred Willfart												
VINTAGE	1945												
	1970												
	1995												
	2020												
WINE TYPE	Assti Spufarte												
	Chartdonhay												
	Pinot Marron												
	Smellion												

WHAT WAS THEIR WINE'S VINTAGE?

WHAT TYPE OF WINE WAS IT?

WHO DID THE POO?

HOW DRUNK WERE THEY?

Suspects	Vintage	Wine Type	Status
Bert Breakwind			
Rebecca Reeks			
Sommelier Stool			
Winifred Willfart			

7. POONIVERSITY STUDIES

Craving a new intellectual challenge, Inspector Poupe has decided to enrol at the Russell Poop Pooniversity. At this prestigious institution, students and academics alike are dedicated to the advancement of human wisdom. In fact, one academic was so absorbed by an intellectual breakthrough that, entirely distracted, they defecated on the floor. So immersed were they that they didn't even notice until Inspector Poupe confronted them. In the spirit of academic rigour, he has matched the four academic suspects to their subject, location and number of degrees, proving their scatty scatological habits once and for all.

SUSPECTS

Her intellect is nearly as big as her stools. Nearly.

AGE 64 – FRENCH – MONOCLE

The unsavoury rumours surrounding him are the most interesting thing about his lectures.

AGE 28 – WELSH – SIDEBURNS

The very model of a nutty poofessor with very nutty poo.

AGE 56 – PORTUGUESE – MOUSTACHE

As cold and hard as a three-day-old stool.

AGE 31 – GERMAN – GLASSES

SUBJECT

Bullshit Studies

It is a real subject, promise!

Diarrhoeal Dialectics

Some highfalutin philosophical shit.

History of Fart

Learn about the most influential fartists of all time.

Poolitical Sciences

Get to the bottom of the political situation.

DEGREES

5

A healthy number, like your five a day.

7

One for each day of the week.

9

A testament to their dedication to avoiding real jobs.

11

So many certificates they might start wiping their arse on them.

LOCATION

Lecture Hall	Old Library
Rows upon rows of benches – perfect for a secret snooze.	Contains the world's oldest collection of poo jokes.

Seminar Room	Study
Where seminal seminars are disseminated.	Piled high with half-empty mugs of tea and half-written papers.

CLUES

- The academic having a snooze on a bench has more degrees than the poolitical scientist.
- The nutty poofessor could have five or 11 degrees. They're so kooky, even they don't remember!
- The highfalutin philosopher does not have enough certificates to wipe their arse on, and neither does the expert on bullshit.
- To really encourage their students' mental stimulation, the university likes to challenge them by publishing the timetable in code: EHT NAMREG CIMEDACA SEHCAET LAEOHRRAID SCITCELAID.
- One academic was perusing the world's oldest collection of poo jokes. They were sniggering to themselves, partly because of the jokes, but also because they had four more degrees than their colleague, Dr. Sewers.
- The academic sat twiddling his moustache had four less degrees than his colleague in the seminar room.
- **The poo was found next to a book on the History of Fart.**

	LOCATION				DEGREES				SUBJECT			
	Lecture Hall	Old Library	Seminar Room	Study	5	7	9	11	Bullshit Studies	Diarrhoeal Dialectics	History of Fart	Poolitical Sciences
SUSPECTS												
Dr. Sewers												
Lecturer Tidswiddle												
Professor Xcrement												
Senior Tooter												
SUBJECT												
Bullshit Studies												
Diarrhoeal Dialectics												
History of Fart												
Poolitical Sciences												
DEGREES												
5												
7												
9												
11												

WHAT IS THEIR SUBJECT?

HOW MANY DEGREES DO THEY HAVE?

WHICH ACADEMIC DID THE POO?

WHERE WERE THEY?

Suspects	Subject	Degrees	Location
Dr. Sewers			
Lecturer Tidswiddle			
Professor Xcrement			
Senior Tooter			

8. PEEK-A-POO!

Poupe attends a parenting support group to offer professional advice on toilet training. While he's there, the group leader makes the attending parents play peekaboo with their babies, stressing the importance of play to raising happy, healthy children. Unfortunately, the excitement is too much for one of the babies. An unbearable stench fills the room – clearly a soiled nappy!

Leaping into action, Poupe works out which baby did the poo, who their parents are and how many peekaboos it took.

SUSPECTS

No matter how often his parents bathe him, Baby Badsmell's peculiar odour remains. Aside from that, he's an adorable baby.

7 MONTHS – 2 TEETH – MALE

Where some babies have teddies, Bogroll has bogroll. She cries and cries unless given a twist of toilet paper to hold.

11 MONTHS – 4 TEETH – FEMALE

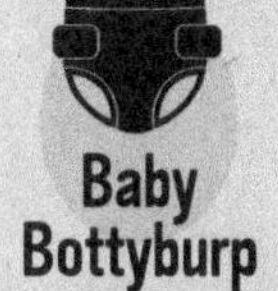

Wee Bottomburp is toilet-trained, so his parents are convinced he fouls his nappies out of spite.

14 MONTHS – 5 TEETH – MALE

Little Brownbib is prone to projectile vomiting and the dreaded 'coming out of both ends'.

9 MONTHS – 3 TEETH – FEMALE

MOTHERS

Mucky Michelle

Michelle is a farmer, so she's often up to her knees in seven flavours of shit. She's determined that her child will grow up as tough as her.

Pungent Polly

With Polly and her husband, it was love at first scent. Motherhood hasn't made her any less smelly.

Spotty Sarah

A young mother with a serious case of acne. Affectionately nicknamed 'the Leopard' by her friends because, despite all the moisturiser, she can't change her spots.

Turdy Trisha

Trisha refused to believe she was pregnant – only bloated – until the moment she went into labour. It was a smooth delivery – the baby couldn't wait to get out.

FATHERS

Arsey Andy

Before becoming a father, he was known as 'Affectionate Andy', but the sleepless nights have turned him into a grump.

Dunny Duncan

Duncan has a lax approach to parenting, perhaps because he wasn't toilet-trained himself until five years old. So long as the baby doesn't poo on his record collection, he's content.

Gross Grant

One may wonder how this bad-smelling, worse-mannered stinkbomb managed to get married and have children. There's someone for everybody, clearly.

Longpoo Lewis

The nickname is self-explanatory. Some of his turds have been mistaken for escaped pythons.

NUMBER OF PEEKABOOS

1	2
A single peekaboo, not that exciting.	Two peekaboos in a row – pretty startling if you're a baby.

3	4
Three peekaboos. By now, the baby should have realised that it's the same face each time.	Four successive peekaboos – the equivalent, for a baby, of watching an action movie.

CLUES

- The nine-month-old baby played peekaboo twice or four times.
- The bad-smelling, worse-mannered stinkbomb only played peekaboo once with his child.
- Ding! Ding! It's that bullshit detector again.

  [See Exhibit C]

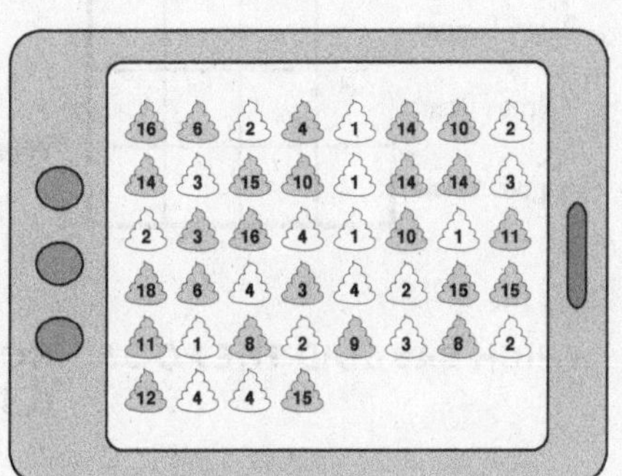

- The group leader passes Poupe a coded message. It reads: "OOPGNOL SIWEL SI TON YBAB S'BIBNWORB REHTAF".
- Spotty Sarah's child played peekaboo two more times than the oldest baby.
- Pungent Polly played peekaboo with her child more times than Dunny Duncan did.
- The number of times the baby with two teeth played peekaboo didn't tally with the number of times the baby with five teeth did.
- **The guilty baby soiled their nappy on the third of three peekaboos.**

		PEEKABOOS				FATHERS				MOTHERS			
		1	2	3	4	Arsey Andy	Dunny Duncan	Gross Grant	Longpoo Lewis	Mucky Michelle	Pungent Polly	Spotty Sarah	Turdy Trisha
SUSPECTS	Baby Badsmell												
	Baby Bogroll												
	Baby Bottyburp												
	Baby Brownbib												
MOTHERS	Mucky Michelle												
	Pungent Polly												
	Spotty Sarah												
	Turdy Trisha												
FATHERS	Arsey Andy												
	Dunny Duncan												
	Gross Grant												
	Longpoo Lewis												

WHO WAS THEIR MOTHER?

WHO WAS THEIR FATHER?

WHICH BABY DID THE POO?

HOW MANY PEEKABOOS DID IT TAKE?

Suspects	Mothers	Fathers	Number of Peekaboos
Baby Badsmell			
Baby Bogroll			
Baby Bottyburp			
Baby Brownbib			

9. ARTIFICIAL INSMELLIGENCE

Inspector Poupe receives an unusual message asking him to come to the office of an up-and-coming tech company. When he arrives, his boss is standing beside a robotic replica of the inspector. "Let me introduce you to Robo-Poupe," he says genially. "He's a cutting-edge artificial intelligence trained on your case files and, if I may say so, it looks like the pupil is going to surpass the master. I've asked four of the employees here to consume a specific fruit and then do their business upon the floor. I want you to figure out who did each poo, their job title, what they ate and how old each stool is. Specifically, I want you to tell me who ate the pineapple. The AI has been given the same task. If you can't beat Robo-Poupe, you're fired!"

SUSPECTS

Dirty Dougal

One of the company's grottiest employees. There's enough dirt under his nails to fill the Grand Canyon.

5'7" – STUDIED CHEMISTRY – BROWN HAIR

Fartacious Fran

Fran considers herself a bit of a wordsmith, hence the fancy-pants nickname. She's also extraordinarily flatulent.

5'6" – STUDIED ENGLISH – BLONDE HAIR

Odo Russ

Odo refuses to change either of his names, saying they define him. He also refuses to wash.

5'11" – STUDIED BIOLOGY – RED HAIR

Toby Turdiano

Turdiano is a natural leader, although his habit of pooing himself when he gets too excited has meant that he hasn't achieved the success he deserves.

5'10" – STUDIED DRAMA – BLACK HAIR

FRUIT

Durian

A thorny fruit with a stenchy interior. Is the sweet taste worth the foul smell?

Mango

A juicy, delicious fruit which pairs well with raisins. Don't swallow the stone.

Pineapple

The only fruit that eats its eater. Enzymes in its juice try to digest your tongue – that's why it tingles.

Watermelon

Poupe checks the stool carefully for any identifying seeds.

JOB TITLE

Binary Translator

In stressful situations, Robo-Poupe sometimes returns to its mother tongue – binary – and an interpreter has to be ready to jump in.

Chief Stool Handler

Sometimes they get through 30 pairs of gloves a day.

Emergency Plumber

Everyone should have an emergency plumber on hand. They're as essential as a fire extinguisher.

Head of Smell Testing

The Head of Smell Testing has taught the AI to recognise over a thousand common smells, from sweet honey to sweaty socks. Will this give it the edge over Poupe?

TIME

One Hour

Because of the laboratory conditions, this turd is practically fresh from the colon. It's a golden-brown colour and as soft as melting ice cream.

Two Hours

This turd has begun to dry up, and a darker brown film has formed over the golden brown. However, it's still just as squashy inside.

Three Hours

After three hours, the turd is mostly dry inside. Thin cracks are beginning to spread over the surface.

Four Hours

This turd has the consistency of freeze-dried ice cream. The wind could blow it away.

CLUES

- The mango turd was two hours old. The watermelon turd was one hour older than the Chief Stool Handler's.
- Robo-Poupe passed its human counterpart a coded message. It read: "HTE AMN WTIH TRYDI IRGAFSEINLN DDI SHI OOP EHRET UHROS GOA".
- The former drama student either handles stools or plumbs toilets.
- Odo Russ was offered a job as Head of Smell Testing but refused, thinking the interviewer was joking: in fairness, the interviewer's name was Jo King.
- The only woman among the suspects did her poo one hour before the Chief Stool Handler.
- The tallest employee didn't eat the durian. They did their poo more than an hour before or after the person who did.
- **Remember, Poupe has been asked to figure out who ate pineapple.**

		TIME				JOB TITLE				FRUIT		
	One Hour	Two Hours	Three Hours	Four Hours	Binary Translator	Chief Stool Handler	Emergency Plumber	Head of Smell Testing	Durian	Mango	Pineapple	Watermelon
SUSPECTS												
Dirty Dougal												
Fartacious Fran												
Odo Russ												
Toby Turdiano												
FRUIT												
Durian												
Mango												
Pineapple												
Watermelon												
JOB TITLE												
Binary Translator												
Chief Stool Handler												
Emergency Plumber												
Head of Smell Testing												

WHAT FRUIT HAD THEY EATEN?

WHAT WAS THEIR JOB TITLE?

WHO DID THE POO?

HOW OLD IS THEIR POO?

Suspects	Fruit	Job Title	Time
Dirty Dougal			
Fartacious Fran			
Odo Russ			
Toby Turdiano			

10. BOTTOMS UP

Of all the weddings he's been to, this is certainly Inspector Poupe's most memorable. A man of faecal facts and reason, he often finds himself drifting off during the sentimental toasts and speeches. Not today. As the gathering raise a glass to the bride, somebody decides to honour the occasion in an altogether different manner by pulling down their trousers and displaying their cheeks for all to see. The bride's dress appears grey next to this pair of gleaming white moons. With the culprit's face obscured, Inspector Poupe must use his detective skills to track them down. After all, the rear end is his department. By matching the partygoers to their drinks, roles and, crucially, their level of drunkenness, the Inspector must find this mooning menace.

SUSPECTS

A filthy man with an even filthier sense of humour.

6'0" – NOVELTY TIE – AGE 48

Skeletons aren't the worst thing you'll find in his closet...

5'9" – PINK TIE – AGE 61

His party trick is farting the national anthem. Strangely, he doesn't get invited to many events.

6'1" – BLUE TIE – AGE 57

Covered in grease from head to toe.

5'7" – RED TIE – AGE 51

DRINK

Champagne

With all that gas inside you, you could do with your own champagne cork.

Gin and Tonic

90% gin and 10% tonic is the perfect ratio for one guest.

Red Wine

A multi-layered drinking experience. Its aroma has powerful bottom notes.

Tequila

A shot of this will make you grimace like the bride's mother.

NUMBER OF DRINKS IN

One

Pleasantly silly and giggly.

Two

The smartest and funniest you've ever been.

Three

Up on the table singing karaoke.

Four

Starting a fight before being bundled into a taxi.

ROLE AT WEDDING

Best Man	Father of The Bride
Could genuinely be the best man at the wedding, not that there's much competition here.	Constantly laments his daughter's terrible taste in men. Where could she have got that from?

Groom	Priest
Everyone admires his beautiful ring.	Despite his job, likes to be the life and soul of the party. Really goes to town at communion.

CLUES

- The best man grimaced after throwing his drink back.
- The groom was ready for a fight when the toasts started.
- The number of champagnes chugged pre-toast was not three.
- The priest consumed two more drinks than the red wine drinker.
- The guest in the novelty tie and the red wine lover were trying to outdrink each other. Their necking was almost neck and neck, with only one drink between them.
- One guest had been doing the rounds with their party trick involving the national anthem, while another mixed themselves some potent G&Ts. Both had been very busy, but one was at least two drinks ahead of the other.
- A drunken guest shouted some garbled message in Inspector Poupe's ear. All he could make out was "EHT REBMUN FO YTPME SESSALGYBYZAELS WETS SI TON EERHT".
- **The person who had drunk the most decided to expose their cheeks.**

		Best Man	Father of The Bride	Groom	Priest	One	Two	Three	Four	Champagne	Gin and Tonic	Red Wine	Tequila
		ROLE AT WEDDING				DRINKS IN				DRINK			
SUSPECTS	Filthy Frankie												
	Ropey Roger												
	Seedy Simon												
	Sleazy Stew												
DRINK	Champagne												
	Gin and Tonic												
	Red Wine												
	Tequila												
DRINKS IN	One												
	Two												
	Three												
	Four												

WHAT WERE THEY DRINKING?

HOW MANY DRINKS HAD THEY HAD?

WHO EXPOSED THEMSELVES?

WHAT WAS THEIR ROLE AT THE WEDDING?

Suspects	Drink	Number Of Drinks In	Role At Wedding
Filthy Frankie			
Ropey Roger			
Seedy Simon			
Sleazy Stew			

11. TOILET HUMOUR

As the old saying goes, it's all shits and giggles until somebody giggles and shits – which is just what happened at the Bar Stool Comedy Night. One comedian took to the stage and, laughing a little too hard at their own joke, promptly soiled themselves. While the audience thought it was the most hilarious thing to happen all night, Inspector Poupe did not find it quite so funny. Detecting the whiff of faeces, he sets about identifying the culprit. By compiling information on each suspect's best joke, comedy style and place on the bill, he soon builds up a profile to help him take this clown down.

SUSPECTS

Joe Pong

He's the poster boy for edgy humour, bravely sticking it to the marginalised social groups.

AGE 43 – SHEFFIELD – GREEN WAISTCOAT

Lou Rolls

The only woman on the bill once again, she has taken to wearing a fake moustache to blend in.

AGE 32 – NORWICH – RED SHIRT

Pee Wee Jones

Not the most sparkling of wits – luckily his regional accent makes anything funny!

AGE 56 – LEEDS – PINK JACKET

Willy Waggle

A cheeky young upstart making a splash on the comedy scene.

AGE 24 – LIVERPOOL – ORANGE SHORTS

BEST JOKE

Wanna Hear My Poo Joke?

Are you sure?
It's a really corny one.

What's Brown And Sticky?

BBQ ribs of course!
What were you thinking?

Why Did The Turd Stay Home?

He was a real party-pooper.
OK, OK, it's a crap joke.

Why Was The Poo Sad?

He just got dumped.
It's probably fair to say he was having a really shit time.

STYLE

Alternative

Sick of comedy you understand?
Try this scatologically surreal alternative.

Deadpan

Not to be confused with bedpan.

Observational

Turns out what they mainly observe is their own toilet habits.

Ventriloquist

Trouser-poopingly sinister to some, pant-wettingly hilarious to others.

ORDER ON THE BILL

First	Second
The most nerve-racking job of all. This act is here to break the ice, but usually ends up breaking wind.	Allegedly the best.

Third	Fourth
The one with the hairy chest.	The headline act! Like the dropping of the log after a preliminary wee.

CLUES

- "He just got dumped!" quipped the third comedian on the bill, as the audience erupted into delirious fits of laughter. It got a much bigger laugh than the previous comedian's joke – some garbage about BBQ ribs.
- The deadpan comedian had to come on straight after the corny poo joke. What an act to follow!
- "HTASW' RNOWB ADN TSIYKC?" the Sheffield comedian slurred at the audience.
- Pee Wee Jones has dabbled in both alternative and observational styles of comedy. He never tells corny jokes.
- The cheeky young comedian appeared on the bill two places after their scatologically surreal colleague.
- **The pooer nearly dropped their ventriloquist's dummy.**

	ORDER ON THE BILL				STYLE				BEST JOKE			
	First	Second	Third	Fourth	Alternative	Deadpan	Observational	Ventriloquist	Wanna Hear My Poo Joke?	What's Brown And Sticky?	Why Did The Turd Stay Home?	Why Was The Poo Sad?
SUSPECTS												
Joe Pong												
Lou Rolls												
Pee Wee Jones												
Willy Waggle												
BEST JOKE												
Wanna Hear My Poo Joke?												
What's Brown And Sticky?												
Why Did The Turd Stay Home?												
Why Was The Poo Sad?												
STYLE												
Alternative												
Deadpan												
Observational												
Ventriloquist												

WHAT WAS THEIR BEST JOKE?

WHAT STYLE OF COMEDY DID THEY PERFORM?

WHO SOILED THEMSELVES?

WHERE DID THEY APPEAR ON THE BILL?

Suspects	Best Joke	Style	Order On Bill
Joe Pong			
Lou Rolls			
Pee Wee Jones			
Willy Waggle			

12. SCARED SHITLESS

On Halloween, four plucky teenagers attend the 'Shite Night' at their local amusement parp. After spending a hour or so on the ordinary rides, they enter the haunted house. As they pass through the darkened cellar, an actor leaps out from behind a creaking door and shakes bloody chains. It's too much for one of the fearless four, who screams and shits themselves. Inspector Poupe promptly attends the call and deduces the identity of the pants-pooer, their costume, what time they are expected home and their favourite ride.

SUSPECTS

Boris Bigshits

A brave boy with big bowels. If he was the shocked shitter, then expect a colossal cleanup.

AGE 15 – EXCLAIMS "WOW!" – FAVOURITE COLOUR IS RED

Christine Crapponit

Christine is rather temperamental, and her kneejerk reaction to any criticism is to release a volley of turds.

AGE 17 – EXCLAIMS "CRAP!" – FAVOURITE COLOUR IS YELLOW

Patricia Poosley

Miss Poosley claims she isn't scared of anything, although if you look closely her knees are shaking.

AGE 16 – EXCLAIMS "YIPES!" – FAVOURITE COLOUR IS BLUE

Vincent Voidbowels

A suave young man with a flair for the dramatic and a vintage charm.

AGE 18 – EXCLAIMS "HOW FRIGHTFUL!" – FAVOURITE COLOUR IS GREEN

COSTUME

Clown

Will do anything to make the others laugh. Does this extend to soiling themselves?

Ghost

White sheets are awful for skid marks.

Vampire

Complete with fake blood dribbling down their cheeks, and fake poo dribbling down their backside.

Werewolf

It can't be pleasant getting dried faeces out of faux fur.

CURFEW

19:00

A seven o'clock curfew is so lame, as the yoof say. Or said. I don't know anymore.

20:00

By eight, it's getting dark. If you don't watch your step while walking home, you could tread on a dog poo.

21:00

Back just in time to watch TV after the watershed.

22:00

A 10 o'clock curfew still feels early when you're a teenager. Most of them will stay up for hours on their mobile phones anyway. In the old days we had to entertain ourselves...

FAVOURITE RIDE

Dodgems	Ferris Wheel
All that bumping and thumping may have hurried the bowels along.	Not recommended for sufferers of vertigo. The stress of being up high could cause sudden evacuation of the bowels.

Helter Skelter	Rollercoaster
An old-fashioned slide on a coconut mat. For those afraid of faster rides.	Its loop-the-loop is also called the 'muck spreader' because riders who poo their pants have their faeces hurled in all directions. That didn't happen to any of Poupe's suspects, but perhaps all the spinning had a knock-on effect?

CLUES

- The teenager who prefers yellow is either dressed as a clown or in faux fur. The Ferris wheel is their favourite ride.
- The teenager who exclaimed "How frightful!" is expected home two hours later than their friend dressed as a ghost.
- The youngest member of the group enjoyed the helter skelter the best. Despite their youth, they're allowed to come home two hours later than the werewolf.
- A horrifying coded message was found daubed on the walls of the haunted house in blood (or possibly red paint). It read, "REVEOHW SEVOL EHT SMEGDOD SI DESOPPUS OT EB KCAB ENO RUOH RETFA EHT REGANEET DESSERD SA A ERIPMAV".
- **There were skid marks on a white sheet.**

		FAVOURITE RIDE				CURFEW				COSTUME			
		Dodgems	Ferris Wheel	Helter Skelter	Rollercoaster	19:00	20:00	21:00	22:00	Clown	Ghost	Vampire	Werewolf
SUSPECTS	Boris Bigshits												
	Christine Crapponit												
	Patricia Poosley												
	Vincent Voidbowels												
COSTUME	Clown												
	Ghost												
	Vampire												
	Werewolf												
CURFEW	19:00												
	20:00												
	21:00												
	22:00												

WHAT WERE THEY DRESSED AS?

WHEN ARE THEY EXPECTED HOME?

WHO DID THE POO?

WHICH WAS THEIR FAVOURITE RIDE?

Suspects	Costume	Curfew	Favourite Ride
Boris Bigshits			
Christine Crapponit			
Patricia Poosley			
Vincent Voidbowels			

13. MAKING A SPLASH

Inspector Poupe tries to keep himself in good shape, knowing that a lack of exercise can often lead to loose bowels in old age. He's swimming a length at his local pool when he overhears a commotion. Someone has defecated on one of the diving boards.

There are four professional swimmers who frequent the pool, and Poupe singles them out immediately. After working out their favourite stroke, their sporting nicknames and the height of the board they leapt from, he points the finger at the dirty diver.

SUSPECTS

Daisy Dogshit

When she isn't in the pool, Daisy can be found playing with her three huge dogs. They're not house-trained, hence her epithet.

7 COMPETITION WINS – WEARS A WETSUIT – BROWN EYES

Jess Justafart

'Justafart' isn't her real surname, but people call her it because of her habit of soiling her swimming costume with what she thought was 'just a fart'.

11 COMPETITION WINS – WEARS A SWIMCAP – GREEN EYES

Murky Mike

Like a squid, Mike leaves a dark trail in the water. Only... this ain't ink.

6 COMPETITION WINS – WEARS FLIPPERS – BROWN EYES

Straining Stuart

Stuart holds in his farts until a crucial moment in the race, then releases for the extra propulsion. He is not well liked.

13 COMPETITION WINS – WEARS GOGGLES – BLUE EYES

FAVOURITE STROKE

Backstroke

The stroke for entitled folk who want others to get out of their way.

Breaststroke

So called because it's the best stroke.

Butterfly

If someone says this is their favourite, they're lying. There's a reason you never see a butterfly swimming underwater.

Front Crawl

The standard stroke, it makes the biggest splash.

NICKNAME

Floater

This swimmer got their name because of their habit of bobbing on the surface of the pool, looking for all the world like a dead fish... or something grosser.

Flusher

So nicknamed because they can shoot to the bottom of the pool faster than anyone else, just as if they were being flushed down a toilet.

Plunger

A nickname given to an avid diver. They're also excellent at unblocking toilets.

Sinker

Sinks like a stone, and swims like one too.

METRES DIVED

Four	Six
It may be the lowest height here, but a fall of four metres can still be shocking if you land flat on your belly. Did it force a turd out?	Your average giraffe is a little shorter than this, so this diving board is not to be sniffed at.

Eight	Ten
A large reticulated python could just about touch this diving board with its tongue while its tail was still in the water. Let's hope there's only people in the pool today.	The international sporting standard. You can dive from higher, though this landlubber doesn't see why you'd want to.

CLUES

- The swimmer dubbed the Floater didn't dive from the 10m board.
- Poupe found a note in the changing rooms. It read: "EHT REHSULF TFEL A KRAD LIART NI EHT RETAW".
- The green-eyed swimmer didn't jump from a height of eight metres.
- The front crawler dived from a board four metres higher than the Sinker's. Likewise, the Floater dived from a board four metres higher than the Plunger's, ironically.
- The wetsuit-wearing swimmer dived from a board four metres lower than the one used by whoever claims butterfly is their favourite stroke.
- After jumping a measly four metres, one of the swimmers did a length of backstroke – their favourite.
- **The turd was found on the highest diving board.**

	Four	Six	Eight	Ten	Floater	Flusher	Plunger	Sinker	Backstroke	Breaststroke	Butterfly	Front Crawl
	METRES DIVED				NICKNAME				FAVOURITE STROKE			
SUSPECTS: Daisy Dogshit												
Jess Justafart												
Murky Mike												
Straining Stuart												
FAVOURITE STROKE: Backstroke												
Breaststroke												
Butterfly												
Front Crawl												
NICKNAME: Floater												
Flusher												
Plunger												
Sinker												

WHAT IS THEIR FAVOURITE STROKE?

WHAT IS THEIR NICKNAME?

WHO DID THE POO?

HOW HIGH WAS THE DIVING BOARD?

Suspects	Favourite Stroke	Nickname	Metres Dived
Daisy Dogshit			
Jess Justafart			
Murky Mike			
Straining Stuart			

14. PRIME TIME SMELLIVISION

From the ingenious minds of our foulest inventors comes a brilliant new invention: smellivision! Bring your favourite shows to life by transporting smells to your home. Inspector Poupe, overjoyed by this breakthrough, rushes to get his hands on this brand new piece of tech. However, one night, as he is flicking through the channels in order from 1 to 4, he is overwhelmed by a disgusting odour – one he is all too familiar with. One of the actors has done a secret poo in their pants, Poupe is sure of it. He must link each actor to their show, their role and the channel they appear on. In doing so, he will find out whose careless pooing is to blame for this foul stench.

SUSPECTS

Amanda Fetor

Renowned beauty, maintains toxic beauty standards by following a strict diet of raw onions.

AGE 28 – GINGER – AUSTRALIAN

Bud Cheeks

He used to make the girls scream; that's before smellivision revealed his halitosis. Now they scream for different reasons.

AGE 35 – BLOND – AMERICAN

Chad Reekster

The quintessential hard man. He's been wearing the same 'aftershave' for years. Turns out it's lady's perfume.

AGE 37 – BUZZ CUT – SCOTTISH

Julie Funk

Looks like a tangerine. The smell of fake tan suggests this might not be 100% natural.

AGE 42 – BRUNETTE – SWEDISH

SHOW

Bottom Bandits

A side-splitting comedy with plenty of funny smells.

Good Poos Gone Bad

The theme tune is catchy, a bit like norovirus.

Know Thy Enema

A cult classic, particularly popular amongst actual cults.

Log Squad

A much-loved lumberjack saga that spans several generations.

CHANNEL

1

The family channel! Home to classics like *Mum, I Did A Poo* and *Saturday Morning Runs*.

2

Dubbed the 'intellectual' channel, they educate and entertain their audience with riveting documentaries like *The Rise and Fall of Doorknobs* and *The Emotional Life of Fungus*, to name but two.

3

The trendy channel that targets 'young people' – only ten years behind the curve!

4

A generally trashy and bizarre mix of conspiracy theories, dating shows and darts, with the odd comedy rerun thrown in.

ROLE

Angry Toilet Attendant	**Constipated Anti-Hero**
In fairness you'd be angry too if you were a toilet attendant.	Played by a method actor who ate nothing but steak for four weeks.
Corrupt Traffic Cop	**Misunderstood Teenager**
Exploring this fine character's story provides a gripping commentary on the issues that matter.	Or are they simply obnoxious? The jury's out.

CLUES

- The comedy show does not feature an angry toilet attendant.
- Inspector Poupe caught a snippet of a cult classic on a higher channel number than that on which he smelt lady's perfume.
- A method actor has no place on a trendy young person's channel.
- As the closing credits on one show sped across the screen, this is all Inspector Poupe could make out: "ADHC RTREEKSE ASYPL HET RDTEDONOSIUSM GETERANE".
- The corrupt traffic cop had appalling halitosis (and probably anal halitosis, too.)
- Julie Funk's tangerine face appeared one channel number lower than that on which the angry toilet attendant appeared.
- Poupe moves to the channel numbered two higher than the one showing the cult classic. He does a little dance when he hears a catchy theme tune.
- **Poupe reckons the scent of poo was strongest during the lumberjack saga.**

		Role: Angry Toilet Attendant	Role: Constipated Anti-Hero	Role: Corrupt Traffic Cop	Role: Misunderstood Teenager	Channel: 1	Channel: 2	Channel: 3	Channel: 4	Show: Bottom Bandits	Show: Good Poos Gone Bad	Show: Know Thy Enema	Show: Log Squad
Suspects	Amanda Fetor												
	Bud Cheeks												
	Chad Reekster												
	Julie Funk												
Show	Bottom Bandits												
	Good Poos Gone Bad												
	Know Thy Enema												
	Log Squad												
Channel	1												
	2												
	3												
	4												

WHAT SHOW ARE THEY IN?

WHAT CHANNEL IS IT ON?

WHO DID THE SECRET POO?

WHO DO THEY PLAY?

Suspects	Show	Channel	Role
Amanda Fetor			
Bud Cheeks			
Chad Reekster			
Julie Funk			

15. POOPIE CUSHION

Mrs. Potty returned from a bathroom break (needs must) to be greeted by the odour of poo wafting from a living room cushion. Evidently one of her quads had had a little accident on the sofa. All four children are recently out of nappies, and so it is paramount Mrs. Potty can identify the culprit so they can be provided with further toilet training. She calls on the services of her trusty neighbour, the esteemed Inspector Poupe, to get to the bottom of it, if you'll pardon the pun. Poupe soon establishes how long each child has been out of nappies, the snack they had consumed and their favourite toy. The identity of the pooper does not remain a mystery for long.

SUSPECTS

Dottie Potty

Dottie has a penchant for all things spotty, which is fortunate given her name. She loves dalmatians, polka dots and cheetahs.

RED HAIR – BLUE EYES – LEFT-HANDED

Lottie Potty

Lottie's full name is Charlotte, but her parents insist she goes by Lottie. No idea why.

BROWN HAIR – HAZEL EYES – RIGHT-HANDED

Mottie Potty

Mottie is a dapper young boy, and insists on always wearing a bow tie. Cute!

BROWN HAIR – HAZEL EYES – RIGHT-HANDED

Scottie Potty

Scottie is the most down-to-earth of the quads. He'll do anything, eat anything and try anything.

BLOND HAIR – BLUE EYES – LEFT-HANDED

FAVOURITE TOY

Bouncy Ball

A chaotic little ball of madness that has been lost over 50 times (that's a ballpark figure). One of the Potty kids loves it dearly.

Car

One of the Potty children loves pushing their brown toy car around the house. Perhaps a car-eer as a mechanic awaits.

Rocking Horse

A rocking horse walks into a bar...

Spaceship

The toy that is marketed as being 'out of this world' is certainly a stellar hit with one of the Potty children. Huzzah!

DAYS OUT OF NAPPIES

7

Always considered a lucky number, but was it unlucky number seven for one of the Potty's today?

14

An accidental number two after a period of two weeks? It couldn't be, could it?

21

Twenty-one is another name for blackjack, but was one of the Potty family playing a different casino game today – craps, perchance?

28

In maths, 28 is called a perfect number. But was it a little less-than-perfect today for one of the Potty's?

SNACK EATEN

Carrot Sticks

Crunchy little sticks of orange goodness. Healthy, to boot. Could you want more?

Cereal

Not known to lead to unexpected bowel movements, but then life is inherently unpredictable.

Scrambled Eggs

Take some eggs, add some milk, whisk a bit, warm up and then wait for the liquid to set. Delicious eggy goodness ensues.

Toast

A classic snack, and rather delicious when devoured with a liberal smear of chocolate spread on top, as was the case for one lucky Potty today.

CLUES

- The bow-tie wearing Potty has been out of nappies for two weeks longer than the Potty who has just eaten some carrot sticks.
- Someone gave Poupe the following garbled note: "HTEYTTOP ICLDH WOH ATE A WOLB FO AEERLC SAH EENB UOT FO PPSNAIE RFO ETHER EESWK".
- The Potty who consumed a delicious eggy snack has been out of nappies for a fortnight.
- The blond-haired Potty has been out of nappies for longer than their sibling who loves playing with a toy car.
- The child who loves riding their rocking horse has not been out of nappies for the longest period of time.
- The Potty family member whose favourite toy has been lost around 50 times has been out of nappies for two weeks less than their sibling who loves all things spotty.
- **There were tiny flecks of cereal in the poo.**

	SNACK EATEN				DAYS OUT OF NAPPIES				FAVOURITE TOY			
	Carrot Sticks	Cereal	Scrambled Eggs	Toast	7	14	21	28	Bouncy Ball	Car	Rocking Horse	Spaceship
SUSPECTS: Dottie Potty												
Lottie Potty												
Mottie Potty												
Scottie Potty												
FAVOURITE TOY: Bouncy Ball												
Car												
Rocking Horse												
Spaceship												
DAYS OUT OF NAPPIES: 7												
14												
21												
28												

WHAT IS THEIR FAVOURITE TOY?

HOW MANY DAYS HAVE THEY BEEN OUT OF NAPPIES?

WHO DID THE POOPIE ON THE CUSHION?

WHAT SNACK DID THEY CONSUME?

Suspects	Favourite Toy	Days Out of Nappies	Snack Eaten
Dottie Potty			
Lottie Potty			
Mottie Potty			
Scottie Potty			

16. SHITSHAPE

Yo ho ho and a bottle of... bum? Inspector Poupe's research into historical toilet habits leads him to a book on the Age of Sail. He reads about a famous scandal aboard a vessel known as the *Golden Hindquarters*. After a fearsome night of carousing, a wet turd was discovered outside the captain's cabin. Although the book claims the case is unsolved, Poupe's investigative acumen allows him to deduce who did the poo, their role on the ship, what they had eaten and how many gallons of grog they had consumed on the week of the accident.

SUSPECTS

Ava Schitt

Ava is foul-mouthed by sailors' standards, which is saying a lot. None of her dialogue is reproducible in print, not even as asterisks.

RED HAIR – TRICORN HAT – 28 VOYAGES

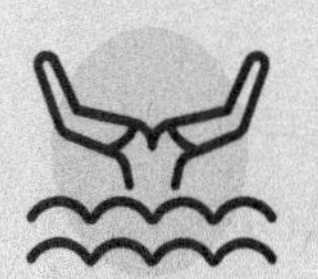

Grace Less

Grace is the clumsiest of sailors, always getting tangled in the rigging or accidentally falling overboard. The other sailors consider her something of a good luck charm. The way they see it, there's only so much shit that can happen, and Grace seems to keep it all to herself.

BLONDE HAIR – BANDANA – 24 VOYAGES

Harold Smellson

Valiant Harold Smellson has a heart of oak but, unfortunately, bowels of paper.

BROWN HAIR – EYE PATCH – 32 VOYAGES

Jack Tar

Known as 'Jolly Jack' because of his frequent inebriation, and 'Tar' because of how often he says "thank you".

BLACK HAIR – RED COAT – 21 VOYAGES

ROLE

Bosun

No, not the atomic particle, silly! It's short for 'boatswain'.

Captain

Aboard the ship, the captain is king. If they did the poo, it's unlikely they'll face any repercussions.

Cook

If the food is bad, the cook can't complain – they prepared it!

First Mate

The first mate is the naval equivalent of a lieutenant and responsible for the day-to-day running of the ship.

FOOD

Corned Beef

The 'corns' are large grains of salt embedded in the meat, not warts. Yummy...

Hard Tack

Tough, tooth-cracking ship's biscuits. Will leave the digestive tract in the same shape that they came in.

Lemons and Limes

Will keep you from getting scurvy, though all that acid could wear your teeth to nubs.

Tinned Pilchards

Oily and delicious. If supply runs low, more can be caught (fish, not tins).

GROG CONSUMED

5	8
Yar! This sailor quaffs a measly five gallons of grog per week. That's 'knot' enough.	Eight gallons of grog will make most sea dogs slightly tipsy, and a landlubber comatose with drink.

11	14
Eleven gallons of grog... you won't be a very able seaman after drinking that.	Fourteen gallons of grog. Yar... that'll make you feel more than a bit groggy.

CLUES

- The sailor in the tricorn hat was either the bosun or the captain.
- Fourteen gallons of grog were necessary to wash down the super-salty corned beef.
- The clumsiest sailor drank the smallest quantity of grog.
- The book mentions a cryptic note found in a treasure chest, which Poupe feels confident he can decipher. It reads: "EHT TSRIF ETAM T'NDID EKATYNA SNOITUACERP TSNIAGA YVRUCS".
- Lemons are mostly liquid, so whoever ate them didn't feel the need to drink as much grog as whoever's diet was hard tack. To be precise, they drank six gallons less.
- The cook guzzled a similar amount of grog to the captain – either three gallons more or three gallons less.
- The sailor with a heart of oak drank six gallons more grog than the first mate.
- **According to Poupe's book, the offending poo "had a most foetid fishy odour".**

	5	8	11	14	Corned Beef	Hard Tack	Lemons and Limes	Tinned Pilchards	Bosun	Captain	Cook	First Mate
	GROG CONSUMED				FOOD				ROLE			
SUSPECTS: Ava Schitt												
Grace Less												
Harold Smellson												
Jack Tar												
ROLE: Bosun												
Captain												
Cook												
First Mate												
FOOD: Corned Beef												
Hard Tack												
Lemons and Limes												
Tinned Pilchards												

WHAT WAS THEIR ROLE ONBOARD?

WHAT HAD THEY EATEN?

WHO DID THE POO?

HOW MUCH GROG HAD THEY DRUNK?

Suspects	Role	Food	Grog Consumed
Ava Schitt			
Grace Less			
Harold Smellson			
Jack Tar			

17. A PAT ON THE BACK

One day, Inspector Poupe is paying a visit to his friend, Farmer Piles. However, their peaceful stroll through the dairy farm is brutally disturbed when Piles slips and falls in a fresh, steaming cowpat. As the flies buzz around the angry farmer, Inspector Poupe promises him revenge. He will work out which member of the herd is behind this monstrosity, stopping at nothing to find the location, age and breed of each bovine suspect. This was another chance to flaunt his detective prowess and by god he was going to milk it.

SUSPECTS

Big Bum Betsy

Her hobbies include chewing grass, passing wind and chewing some more grass.

GOLD – LOVES GRASS – BOUGHT AT MARKET

Moody Judy

Unless you want a hoof to the head, it's best not to mess with her.

BROWN – LOVES A FIGHT – REARED FROM BIRTH

Mother Udders

A warm and bubbly personality, she could happily moo away to the other cows all day long.

BLACK – LOVES A CHAT – STOLEN

Smelly Ellie

Easily identified by the cloud of flies hovering around her.

WHITE – LOVES DAYDREAMING – RESCUED

AGE IN YEARS

3

Still in a playful, naive stage of life. Oblivious to the woes of the bovine world.

4

This cow is in its edgy teenage phase. It battles its angst by listening to heavy metal cowbells and smoking daisies.

5

This cow has entered a full-blown midlife crisis. Catch it speeding around on tractors and chatting up the young heifers.

6

The oldest and wisest member of the herd, it is content just chewing the cud.

BREED

Aberdeen Anguffs

Too cute to eat... almost.

Gassy Highland

Long hair and warming farts equip them for the harsh climate of the Scottish Highlands.

Jersey Farter

Produce deliciously creamy milk and even creamier pats.

Methane Friesian

With the quantity of emissions they produce, it's hard to believe they've only got four stomachs.

LOCATION

Haystack	Lily Pond
The ideal place to look for needles.	What draws cows to this spot is not the brightly plumed ducks, nor the beautiful aquatic flowers, but the chance to admire their own reflection.

Meadow	Old Oak Tree
Filled with buttercups – frolicking is irresistible here.	Do cows sit or stand when it's about to rain? The smart ones get under a tree.

CLUES

- The daydreamer produces deliciously creamy milk.
- The member of the herd that loves a chat is older than the frolicking cow.
- The Methane Friesian is going through its edgy teenage phase.
- One cow thought it was about to rain, so went to take shelter under the old oak tree. Its friend, who was two years younger, wasn't bothered: it was built to withstand a harsh climate.
- The cow of a long-haired breed does not care for frolicking.
- The brown cow was hanging around either the haystack or the meadow.
- Farmer Piles' son witnessed the whole sorry affair. His spelling leaves something to be desired, but he did his best to help by noting down what he saw: 'EHT WOC GNIHCRAES HGUORHT EHT KCATSYAH SI ENO RAEY REDLO NAHT EHT NEEDREBA SFFUGNA'.
- **When he received the pat on the back, Farmer Piles was surrounded by cackling ducks.**

		LOCATION				BREED				AGE IN YEARS		
	Haystack	Lily Pond	Meadow	Old Oak Tree	Aberdeen Anguffs	Gassy Highland	Jersey Farter	Methane Friesian	3	4	5	6
SUSPECTS: Big Bum Betsy												
Moody Judy												
Mother Udders												
Smelly Ellie												
AGE IN YEARS: 3												
4												
5												
6												
BREED: Aberdeen Anguffs												
Gassy Highland												
Jersey Farter												
Methane Friesian												

HOW OLD ARE THEY?

WHAT BREED ARE THEY?

WHO DID THE COW PAT?

WHERE WERE THEY?

Suspects	Age In Years	Breed	Location
Big Bum Betsy			
Moody Judy			
Mother Udders			
Smelly Ellie			

18. SKID MARKS

Being a racing car driver is one of the most dangerous jobs in the world. However, one of the risks that many ignore, as they watch their heroes skid around corners, is the danger of unexpected poos. Inspector Poupe knows all too well the effect these high speeds can have on your insides. When the inevitable happens and a racer soils their seat, the inspector begins building his case. He matches each driver to their car, their sponsor and their position in the race.

SUSPECTS

Gastro Whizz

His rapid – often unexpected – bowel movements could rival the speed of the fastest sports car.

AGE 32 – RED CAR – 15 INCH NECK

Rod Flash

Racing's number one heart-throb. Looking directly at his teeth may cause blindness.

AGE 28 – SILVER CAR – 14 INCH NECK

Squeaky Wheels

So called thanks to his high-pitched voice and squeaky farts.

AGE 24 – WHITE CAR – 18 INCH NECK

Turbo Turds

An Irishman with a reputation for finishing third. Could today finally be his big win?

AGE 27 – BLUE CAR – 17 INCH NECK

POSITION

First

An excuse to shower in champagne.

Second

Victory slipped through their fingers like diarrhoea.

Third

At least it's not last.

Fourth

Nice guys finish last – not this time however.

CAR MODEL

Crease Lightning

It's systematic, it's hydromatic, it's also a bit whiffy.

Fartmobile

Speedy but emits the most foul-smelling exhaust fumes.

Krappwagen

A carbon neutral model running purely on faeces. The future is now, thanks to science!

Muck Machine

Every man's dream car. It's the must-have accessory for any midlife crisis.

SPONSOR

Commodes And Co

A popular manufacturer of toilets and chocolate bars.

Le Merdier

A producer of distinctive fragrances.

Soggi Arce Ltd

The world's biggest designer brand. The Soggi Arce logo can push a T-shirt's value into the millions.

Wet Wipes Inc

Fashions may come and go, but we will always want wet wipes. An unstoppable business model.

CLUES

- Racing's number one heart-throb ended the day being showered in champagne.
- Ding! Ding! A new message has appeared on the bullshit detector's screen:

  [See Exhibit C]

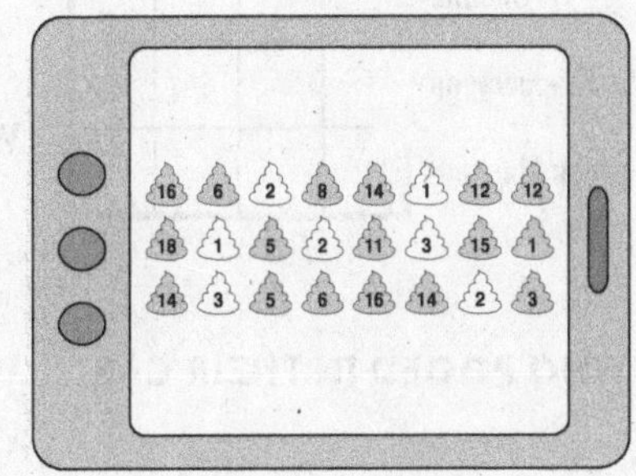

- A car raced one place ahead of Turbo Turds. It was moving at such speed that all he could make out of the branding was: 'EL IERDRME'. Meanwhile the Fartmobile sped along right on the tail of Commodes and Co's driver.
- The driver of the dream car was not sponsored by a fragrance company.
- Rod Flash does not drive a hydromatic car.
- The Muck Machine zoomed along two places ahead of Soggi Arce's driver.
- **Skid marks were found on the Fartmobile's seats.**

		SPONSOR				CAR MODEL				POSITION			
		Commodes And Co	Le Merdier	Soggi Arce Ltd	Wet Wipes Inc	Crease Lightning	Fartmobile	Krappwagen	Muck Machine	First	Second	Third	Fourth
SUSPECTS	Gastro Whizz												
	Rod Flash												
	Squeaky Wheels												
	Turbo Turds												
POSITION	First												
	Second												
	Third												
	Fourth												
CAR MODEL	Crease Lightning												
	Fartmobile												
	Krappwagen												
	Muck Machine												

WHAT PLACE DID THEY FINISH?

WHAT MODEL DID THEY DRIVE?

WHO POOED IN THEIR CAR?

WHO SPONSORED THEM?

Suspects	Position	Car Model	Sponsor
Gastro Whizz			
Rod Flash			
Squeaky Wheels			
Turbo Turds			

19. HOME IS WHERE THE FART IS

Graham's flat stinks of farts. He feels at home amongst the smells of his own rectum and, in fact, rather likes them. One day, however, he notices a new, unfamiliar smell. He sniffs angrily. That's not my fart, he thinks. Enraged, Graham enlists the help of Inspector Poupe to find the culprit. He begins by knocking at number 10, then the next door down (number 11), then the next, until he has matched each resident to the smell and sound of their farts. Inspector Poupe will soon have this gassy house guest in his grasp.

SUSPECTS

Little Jimmy Ripper

Graham's mischievous young nephew – just recently toilet trained.

AGE 6 – BLOND HAIR – BLUE EYES

Old Mrs. Trumpton

A kindly old widow, visits Graham partly for his company but mostly for the free lunch.

AGE 74 – WHITE HAIR – HAZEL EYES

Rosie Gusts

An experimental artist, smashing taboos by using her own poo as a binding agent in her paint. She also does Graham's decorating.

AGE 29 – GINGER HAIR – GREEN EYES

Tod Trumpets

A struggling jazz musician still unaware that, where he lives, nobody likes jazz.

AGE 33 – BROWN HAIR – BROWN EYES

SCENT OF FART

Cabbage

Already smells like farts anyway.

Curry

Is that bhuna?
Smells quite tasty.

Egg

The quintessential fart fragrance.

Spam

A distinctive meaty scent that drives dogs wild.

FLAT NUMBER

10

The bathroom is reportedly haunted by a ghost that died on the toilet. The sheer embarrassment won't let their spirit rest.

11

Used to belong to a local serial pooer, but finally made its way back on the market after a thorough deep clean.

12

Yes, the balcony might overlook the bins – but a balcony's a balcony, OK?

13

A characterful, unique piece of real estate. You get used to the smell of drains after a while.

SOUND OF FART

Squeak	**Squelch**
You would think they had a mouse in their trousers, but fear not, no animals were harmed in the making.	A worryingly wet noise for a fart...
Toot	**Whistle**
A musically talented anus, tooting out groovy trumpet-like sounds.	A disarmingly tuneful melody.

CLUES

- The inhabitant of number 13 does not have tasty-smelling farts.
- The producer of cabbagey guffs lives one door down from the artist.
- The spam farter often hears tooting sounds from two doors up. Little Jimmy Ripper hears the trumpet-like sounds one door up from him.
- Somebody overheard their neighbour gossiping about the struggling musician. All they could make out through the wall was this: "SIH STRAF ERA YKAEUQS DNA LLEMS FO YRRUC".
- The eldest resident produces either worryingly wet-sounding farts or fun trumpet-like ones.
- **Graham's flat had taken on an unpleasant eggy smell.**

		SOUND OF FART				FLAT NUMBER				SCENT OF FART			
		Squeak	Squelch	Toot	Whistle	10	11	12	13	Cabbage	Curry	Egg	Spam
SUSPECTS	Little Jimmy Ripper												
	Old Mrs. Trumpton												
	Rosie Gusts												
	Tod Trumpets												
SCENT OF FART	Cabbage												
	Curry												
	Egg												
	Spam												
FLAT NUMBER	10												
	11												
	12												
	13												

WHAT DID THEIR FART SMELL OF?

WHICH FLAT DID THEY LIVE IN?

WHO FARTED IN GRAHAM'S HOUSE?

WHAT SOUND DID THEIR FART MAKE?

Suspects	Scent of Fart	Flat Number	Sound of Fart
Little Jimmy Ripper			
Old Mrs. Trumpton			
Rosie Gusts			
Tod Trumpets			

20. HOOK, LINE AND STINKER

Let's face it: fishing isn't so different from watching television, only the screen's wet. You sit, you watch, and you wait. But what happens if you set up your foldable chair nowhere near a public toilet? Shit happens, that's what, and Inspector Poupe is never far away. In this case, one of the anglers shat themselves while reeling a fish in. It was a big one, too. Poupe employs his remarkable reasoning powers to deduce who did the poo, how many and what type of fish they caught and what bait they used.

SUSPECTS

Fishy Fiona

Even when she fails to catch anything, Fiona's fishy aroma is never absent. Some suggest it's her shampoo.

AGE 31 – BROWN HAIR – SMELLS LIKE FISH

Rude Rod

A foul-mouthed fisherman who swears even louder if you call him Rodney.

AGE 52 – RED HAIR – SMELLS LIKE TOBACCO

Salty Samuel

Once crew on a trawler, Samuel's spent so long at sea that the salt has soaked into his bones... and possibly his bowels.

AGE 62 – GREY HAIR – SMELLS LIKE SALT

Thomas Tackle

Not to be crossed, since he's also a rugby player. If anyone's in Tom's spot on the river, he unceremoniously shoves them aside.

AGE 28 – BROWN HAIR – SMELLS LIKE SWEAT

FISH TYPE

Carp

Or should that be 'crap'? It is a brown fish, after all.

Minnow

The smallest fish, there's not much for eating on one of these puny things. You'd need to consume at least twenty to make a decent-sized turd.

Pike

This fish has a whopping jaw and tombstone teeth. Don't let it nip you on the bottom.

Salmon

The king of river fish, its greasy skin is sure to lubricate your turds.

NUMBER OF FISH

1

Should've just stayed at home and tried catching fish fingers with some string and a hook.

3

A satisfactory haul. But nothing to make a splash about.

5

Five salmon is an impressive catch. Five minnows? That's small fry.

7

Consistently catch this many fish, and the others might think there's something fishy going on.

BAIT

Earthworms

Raw and wriggling –
a fish's delight.

Maggots

The maggots would eat the fish if they could, so it's only fair.

Old Socks

Apparently some fish are attracted to the cheesy smell clinging to the fabric.

Stale Bread

Once it's in the river, the hardness doesn't matter.

CLUES

- Somebody used earthworms as bait for salmon. They succeeded in catching four more fish than the female suspect.
- One of the anglers left Poupe a message in a bottle, but water seeped in. When he unrolled it, it read: "EHT RELGNA HTIW DER RIAH T'NDID HCTAC A PRAC".
- Whoever used their crusty old socks as bait had a larger haul than the pike-catcher.
- Ding! Ding! As if by magic, Poupe's bullshit detector came to life one last time:

  [See Exhibit C]

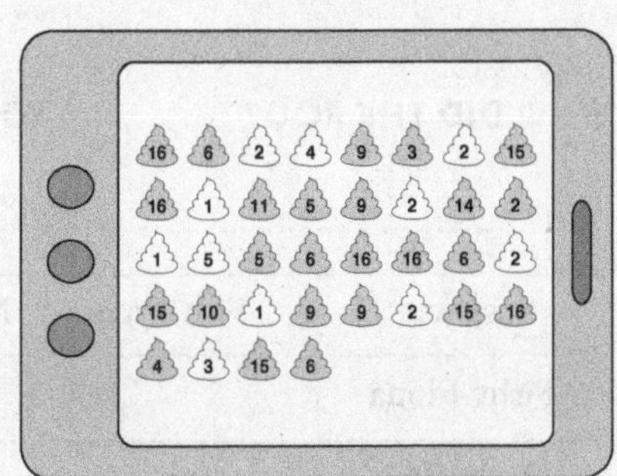

- The stale bread was surprisingly effective bait. Whoever used it caught four more fish than whoever was catching minnows.
- **The turd was found next to a freshly caught carp.**

		BAIT				NUMBER OF FISH				FISH TYPE			
		Earthworms	Maggots	Old Socks	Stale Bread	1	3	5	7	Carp	Minnow	Pike	Salmon
SUSPECTS	Fishy Fiona												
	Rude Rod												
	Salty Samuel												
	Thomas Tackle												
FISH TYPE	Carp												
	Minnow												
	Pike												
	Salmon												
NUMBER OF FISH	1												
	3												
	5												
	7												

WHAT TYPE OF FISH DID THEY CATCH?

HOW MANY FISH DID THEY CATCH?

WHO DID THE POO?

WHAT BAIT DID THEY USE?

Suspects	Fish Type	Number of Fish	Bait
Fishy Fiona			
Rude Rod			
Salty Samuel			
Thomas Tackle			

ANSWERS

EASY 1

Suspects	Dinner	Location
Dr. Dung	Sweetcorn	Living Room
Lady Lav	Cheese	Garden
Mr. Manure	Fish	Kitchen

Mr Manure did a poo in the kitchen! He ate fish, and we can smell it!
"Lies!" the foul old farmer growls before his landlord presents him with a bill for deep cleaning. When he refuses to pay, his stash of special 'compost' is seized by the bailiffs. Bad luck!

EASY 2

Suspects	Lunch	Reactions
Chef Derriere	Cup of Coffee	Blank Stare
Joe Bogs	Tomato Soup	Smile
Suzie Stinkman	Steak Frites	Licking Lips

Chef Derriere was the coffee-drinking poopetrator. He watched Askwhiff take a bite out of the pie with a cold, blank stare.
After interrogation from Inspector Poupe, it transpires that, enraged by Lord Askwhiff's rudeness, he decided to give his dessert some extra coffee flavour.

"If he wants to treat people like crap, he might as well taste some," grumbles the chef as he is served his redundancy notice.

EASY 3

Suspects	Location	Snack Eaten
Belle	Table 2	Chocolate Bar
Danielle	Table 3	Popcorn
Giselle	Table 1	Crisps

Danielle was the mystery farter.
She'd hoped to get away with it, as it was the silent but deadly type, but nothing gets past Inspector Poupe. As he strolled out of the venue, another case solved, he drowned out the sound of Danielle sobbing as she was thrown out of the prestigious event. After all, as everyone knows: you do the crime, you do the time.

EASY 4

Suspects	Receptacle	Drug
Dr. Squatson	A Deerstalker Hat	Tobacco
No Shit Sherlock	A Policeman's Helmet	Cocaine
Professor Morifarty	An Empty Perambulator	Opium

It was Professor Morifarty, the opium addict, who defecated in the empty perambulator.
"No shit Sherlock!" Holes exclaims. He grapples with Morifarty, and the two of them fall tragically into an open septic tank, only to mysteriously reappear several years later. Some things are just too bizarre to make up.

EASY 5

Suspects	Food	Location
Ben Dover	Tuna Sandwich	Under The Trees
Cub Crud	Baked Beans	By The Fire
Sticky Stu	Hot Chocolate	By The Fence

It was Cub Crud by the fire, after eating a can of baked beans!
The poor cub scout immediately bursts into tears. Embarrassed, the scoutmaster pats him on the shoulder. His hand comes away stained.

EASY 6

Suspects	Consistency	Diet
Bear	Gloopy	Beef
Crocodile	Flaky	Salmon
Lion	Smooth	Chicken

It's the lion on a chicken diet!
When Inspector Poupe leaves, the keepers have cancelled their orders of beef and salmon and arranged for a huge delivery of chicken. One month later, the beef-starved bear smashes a hole in its enclosure and rampages through the zoo.

EASY 7

Suspects	Location	Wiped With
Colonel Musturd	Kitchen	Tissue
Mrs. Wipe	Billiard Room	Scarf
Professor Bum	Lounge	Newspaper

Professor Bum was the guilty pooer. He hoped his little gift might liven the party up a bit. The soiled newspaper was also a nice touch too, he thought.
Inspector Poupe strongly disagreed. He soon reprimanded the Professor and left the other guests to enjoy a more civilised evening.

EASY 8

Suspects	Nightwear	Dinner
Ploppy	Dressing Gown	Spaghetti Bolognese
Skidder	Underwear	Mushroom Risotto
Stinky	Pyjamas	Roast Chicken

Stinky's sleepwalking must have got things moving. When he got back into bed, he immediately relieved himself. He did his best to conceal the evidence by hiding his pyjama bottoms, but to no avail.
Inspector Poupe soon sniffed out the culprit, as well as a strong whiff of chicken.

EASY 9

Suspects	Food	Location
Canon Caca	Chocolate Teacakes	By The Font
The Stinking Bishop	Jam Sandwich	By The Altar
Vicar Viscous	Communion Wafers	In The Cloister

It was Canon Caca, by the font, after eating the chocolate teacakes!
The Stinking Bishop is enraged. "In the name of the Holy Ghost, I excommunicate and anathematise you!" he rasps. Terrified, Canon Caca flees, only to slip on his own turd. He is retrieved from the font and sent to the ecclesiastical court for punishment.

EASY 10

Suspects	Emblem	Clothing
Sir Crapsalot	A Turd Issuant	Garderobe
Sir Galahadashit	A Bogbrush Rampant	Chain mail
Sir Pooceval	A Toilet Couchant	Plate armour

It was Sir Pooceval, the Knight of the Can, in his plate armour!
Poupe fancies that Sir Pooceval was probably cast into the dungeon and wasn't even allowed to change his overflowing armour first. What a (k)night.

EASY 11

Suspect	Food	Crime
Dirty Dan	Bread and Water	Public Urination
Foul Flo	Porridge	Drink Driving
Pongy Pete	Mystery Meat	Hooliganism

It was Foul Flo, the drink driver!
As punishment, Flo is put on a bread-and-water diet with Dan. Her refuse no longer looks like porridge, but the odour does not abate.

EASY 12

Suspects	Location	Poo Aroma
Dash	Koi Pond	Dog Food
Flappy	Sundial	Offal
Squawky	Tropical Greenhouse	Burnt Toast

Flappy was the crow who defiled the sundial! Naughty bird.
"Another case cracked with ease!" chuckles Inspector Poupe, pocketing a thick wedge of £20 notes from Lord Chewlip as he exits the property.

EASY 13

Suspects	Ice Cream Flavour	Occupation
Cameron	Strawberry	Dentist
Robin	Chocolate	Preschool Teacher
Terry	Vanilla	Accountant

It was Terry, the accountant, eating vanilla ice cream! Terry is inconsolable after learning their friends have become an item. Robin and Cameron buy them an enormous sundae to cheer them up, but the tears keep flowing... and so does the poo.

EASY 14

Suspects	Location	Wiped With
Barrister Bothamley	Bin	Socks
Hugh Janus Esquire	Garden	Legal Documents
Judge Doodie	Toilet	Banknote

Hugh Janus Esquire was carrying the documents in his briefcase. When he had finished his business in the garden, he grabbed the first paper he could find. Inspector Poupe escorts the disgraced Hugh Janus from the building. Court is adjourned.

EASY 15

Suspects	Toilet	Dinner
Sasha Shartman	Downstairs	Beetroot Soup
Sergio Poorez	Upstairs	Chickpea Stew
Turdie Brown	Loft	Spinach Pie

Sergio blocked the upstairs toilet with his colossal creation. The fibre from the chickpeas had created a monster.
"Time to finish what you started," says Inspector Poupe, as he hands Sergio a plunger.

EASY 16

Suspects	Location	Political Cause
Freedump Fighter	International Bank	Tax Imaginary Friends
Poshitical Activist	Town Square	Legalise Time Travel
SJWC	Government Building	Votes for Dogs

It was the Freedump Fighter who launched a turd at a banker's head, in the name of taxing imaginary friends.
"Make them pay!" was Freedump's rallying cry, as Inspector Poupe snapped on the handcuffs.

EASY 17

Suspects	Last Ate	Last Drank
Brigadier Bowel	French Onion Soup	Tea
Colonel Colon	Sushi	Red Wine
Major Midden	Ham and Egg	Orange Juice

It was Colonel Colon, after a meal of sushi and red wine! The miserable Colon is court-martialled and then sent to the Hague to stand trial on charges of using a biological weapon. He is found guilty and incarcerated for the rest of his life.

EASY 18

Suspects	Last Touched	Wiping Technique
Bob Logs	Door Handle	Flat
Di Rea	Light Switch	Scrunch
Winnie Pooh	TV Remote Control	Fold

Bob Logs had the poonail. The flat toilet paper lacked structural integrity and his finger burst straight through. When he opened the door, his doings were smeared on the already filthy handle.
"I've got a meeting to go to!" huffs the businessman, as Inspector Poupe fetches the soap and water and instructs him to sing 'Happy Birthday' several times over whilst he washes.

EASY 19

Suspects	Location	Motive
Baby Loo Loo	Showers	Fun
Daddy Doo Doo	Pool	Hates Swimming
Grandma Gastro	Changing Rooms	Accident

Daddy Doo Doo was behind the floating faeces. He really does hate swimming.
As Inspector Poupe points an incriminating finger, Daddy Doo Doo turns a bright shade of scarlet. There is nothing he can do but hang his head in shame.

EASY 20

Suspects	Part	Location
Ian	Polonius	Centre Stage
Laurence	King Claudius	Stage Right
Mark	Hamlet	In The Wings

It was Laurence, playing King Claudius, stage right!
The veteran actor begins to blubber. He'd tried so, so hard to keep his sphincter screwed shut, but age was against him. He couldn't help himself. It just poured out.

The show must go on: a change of tights, and he's ready for the next scene. Still, it's more *Shamlet* than *Hamlet*.

MEDIUM 1

Suspects	Surname	Runs Scored	Teatime Snack
Drew	Dunny	13	Tuna Sandwich
Jack	Smellie	0	Beans On Toast
John	Longbottom	87	Sausage Roll
Louie	McWhiffy	111	Scotch Egg

The star bowler, Jack Smellie, made his whites turn brown! Those beans on toast have a lot to answer for. His performance today was far from stellar. Feeling an ominous rumbling in his stomach, he got out for a duck on purpose and walked quickly to the changing room. He almost made it to the toilet... almost, but not quite. Poupe points the finger in his direction – not fessing up to a crime such as this? It's just not cricket.

MEDIUM 2

Suspects	Relationship Status	Food Intolerance	Last Meal
Emma Bidet	Complicated	Dairy	Cheeseburger
Kate Colon	Single	Onion	Margherita Pizza
Lisa Bogroll	Divorced	Tomato	Salade Niçoise
Megan McTurdy	Married	Wheat	Penne Arrabiata

Lisa Bogroll, the divorcee, is thankfully not pregnant. Her salade niçoise contained several pieces of tomato, resulting in severe gas and bloating.
"Worth every bite!" she tells Inspector Poupe, who simply shakes his head at this disgusting fraudster.

MEDIUM 3

Suspects	Location	Score	Club
Caddie Flicht	Rough	Eagle	Wood
Colonel Bogey	Fairway	Par	Iron
Graham Garlick	Green	Birdie	Putter
Will Whiffgift	Bunker	Bogey	Wedge

Graham Garlick did the deed! The grass-grazing golfer is putting on the green when Inspector Poupe apprehends him.
"Enjoy this birdie of yours," he growls, "It'll be your last."

Once Garlick's been frogmarched away, the referee asks Poupe how they can possibly stop this from happening again. The inspector scratches his chin. "Install a public toilet on the course," he says.

MEDIUM 4

Suspects	Favourite Racecourse	Jockey	Racing Colours
Bronx Cheer	Poomarket	Will Whip	Brown Sleeves
Stool Time	Fartwell Park	Brenda Bridle	Beige
Tinkle Toes	Ripoon	Gary Gallop	Dark Brown Spots
Top Scat	Asscot	Clive Canter	Chocolate Hoops

It was Bronx Cheer, the Poomarket-loving horse being ridden by brown-sleeved Will Whip!
Known for passing prodigious amounts of wind, nerves got the better of the poor horse as he was paraded around the ring pre-race. The next thing he knew, there was a steaming crap beneath his feet.

"It's always the dark horse," Poupe chuckles to himself as he saunters cheerfully out of the parade ring to place his bet.

MEDIUM 5

Suspects	Location	Motive	Stool Type
Mickey Bumholes	Supermarket	Cruelty	Runny
Mucky Mel	Library	A Prank	Sausage-like
Pongy Paul	Playground	Revenge	Fluffy
Rancid Rachel	Garden Centre	Desperation	Enormous

Mickey Bumholes is a cruel and twisted individual. He pulled down his trousers and did a runny poo all over the supermarket floor, cackling maniacally as he did so.
"I don't regret a thing," he tells Inspector Poupe, a chilling glint in his eye.

MEDIUM 6

Suspects	Instrument	Band	Song
Ava Hole	Drums	Electric Turd	In the Groove
Billy Pumps	Keyboard	The Splash	I Want Poo
Sid Chunks	Bass	Stall Rockers	Your Pong
Zoe Wee	Lead Guitar	Touching Cloth	Brown River

Rather fittingly, the keyboard player, Billy Pumps, soiled himself performing 'I Want Poo' with The Splash.
Inspector Poupe can't help but hum the chorus as he collects Billy's soiled leather trousers.

MEDIUM 7

Suspects	Superpowers	Nemesis	Evil Plan
Incontinent Isaiah	Telekinesis	Loocifer	Block The Sewers
Miss Mist	Super Strength	The Turdinator	Prevent Litter Collection
Pooperman	Pyrokinesis	Kami-Khazi	Hack Into Your Toilet
Skunk-Man	Telepathy	Porcellana	Pump Sewage Into Ocean

It was Miss Mist, the super-strong superhero!
"Mist!" Mist swears as she's taken in for questioning.
Her superhero licence is revoked, and she ends up working in insurance. One year later, the Turdinator destroys the last bin lorry, ushering in an era of uncollected litter. Civilisation returns to the cave-dwelling stage, only now people dwell within hollowed-out mountains of rubbish.

MEDIUM 8

Suspects	Location	Tool	Artefact
Dr. Dumps	Beach	Shovel	Pottery Shards
Lady Logs	Woodland	Pitchfork	Coin
Professor Squits	Hillside	Spade	Jewellery
Sir Poopster	Field	Trowel	Arrowhead

Dr. Dumps brought her shovel to the beach, where she unearthed some extremely unusual pottery shards. Surely enough to make any self-respecting archaeologist produce a bum sausage.
Inspector Poupe marvels at the discovery of the rare pottery whilst patting himself on the back for being the world's number one at sniffing out number twos.

MEDIUM 9

Suspects	Location	Sandcastle Type	Sand Type
Betty Bowles	Shitby	Moated	Shingle
John Quincy	Wastings	Walled	Mud
Kathryn Krapper	Robin Hood's Bog	Heaped	Dry Sand
Malcolm Moreshit	Gryme Regis	Fancy	Wet Sand

Kathryn Krapper is the culprit! She tried to hide her shit under a heaped, dry-sand sandcastle on the shores of Robin Hood's Bog.
The turd washes up on the beach the next day and is trodden on by a surfer.

MEDIUM 10

Suspects	Food	Reason	Times Flushed
Blocked-Up Barbara	Probiotic Yoghurt	Too Much Sitting	1
Can't-Shit Sally	Rhubarb Crumble	Not Enough Fibre	4
Costive Connor	Chocolate Milk	Dehydration	2
No-Dung Norbert	Jar Of Prunes	Held It In	3

Blocked-Up Barbara's turd stank of yoghurt and despite her sedentary lifestyle, it only had to be flushed once! She wasn't constipated at all!
"I don't understand," says the bemused inspector. "Why would you choose to be known as 'Blocked-Up Barbara'?"

"It's better than the alternative," says Barbara. She tells him. It is.

MEDIUM 11

Suspects	Arrived By	Food	Stool Shape
Grey	Teleportation	Freeze-Dried Ice Cream	Log
Little Green Man	Crashed Spaceship	Hamburger	Cube
Reptilian	Meteor	Vegetables	Torus
Space Bug	Flying Saucer	Turkey	Sphere

The Reptilian alien had been holding it in ever since it crawled out of the meteor! Its torus-shaped stool stank strongly of vegetables.

Men in black apprehend the lizardman after a fierce struggle. For breaking intergalactic law, it's sentenced to a thousand years frozen in ice. After being thanked for his service, Inspector Poupe is routinely mind-wiped. You're next...

MEDIUM 12

Suspects	Subject	Food	Drink
Bea Esse	Episstemology	Scotch Egg	Red Wine
Dr. Drivel	Anthropoology	Potato Salad	Water
Fulla Schitt	Shiterary Theory	Tempura	White Wine
Professor Poupe	Escatology	Cocktail Sausage	Champagne

It was Dr. Drivel, the anthropoologist!

Potato salad and water was enough to turn his delicate stomach. Drivel's colleagues gleefully exult in his humiliation. However, he has tenure, so he's all right.

MEDIUM 13

Suspects	Location	Breed	Category Entered
Angel	Hurdle	Lavrador	Nicest Coat
Buddy	Podium	German Shepturd	Waggiest Tail
Karma	Balance Beam	Shit tzu	Cutest Eyes
Maverick	Tunnel	Poodle	Best Trick

Don't be fooled by those cute eyes! Karma, the shit tzu, did the poo by the balance beam. Perhaps the sight of the tricky obstacle tipped her over the edge. Naughty doggie!
"Quit yapping!" Poupe says to the dog's owner, who continues to protest Karma's innocence whilst being bundled out of the event.

MEDIUM 14

Suspect	Curry	Side Dish	Drink
Gary Guffs	Prawn Madras	Samosa	Lager
Johnny Nugs	Lamb Vindaloo	Onion Bhaji	Red Wine
Shazza Thongs	Chicken Bhuna	Pilau Rice	Vodka
Windy Wendy	Vegetable Phaal	Naan	Stout

The prawn madras, along with the samosa and endless lager, was all too much for Gary Guffs. He stunk the place out and ruined his best pair of jeans.
"Should've stuck to the korma," chuckles Inspector Poupe, as he whisks Gary away to the power shower.

MEDIUM 15

Suspects	Adoptive Family	Crime	Food
Kitty Shat	Stinker	Spat Up A Hairball	Wet Cat Food
Shabby Tabby	Fowles	Scratched The Sofa	Catnip Biscuits
Turdles	Gassmann	Urinated On The Carpet	Fish
Weelix	Aynous	Brought In A Mouse	Dry Cat Food

Weelix is the sinner! The Aynous family returned him after he brought in a mouse and pooed on their carpet. The dry cat food didn't agree with him, clearly.
"Oh, Weelix, not again!" the owner of the rescue centre murmurs. As she picks up the cat to hug him, he piddles on her shoulder.

MEDIUM 16

Suspects	Location	Breakfast	Scent
Doug Shit	Bedroom	Boiled Eggs	Rafflesia Rapture
Gytha Shit	Kitchen	Croissant	Odour de Toilette
Jack Shit	Living Room	Yoghurt	Odour de Colon
Noah Shit	Bathroom	Banana	Civet Oil

It was Noah Shit, the banana-eater!
The three other Shits are quick to denounce their brother. He protests it was just a prank, but that doesn't stop him from being banned for life from this furniture chain. A few days later, he posts the video online and gets millions of views.

MEDIUM 17

Suspects	Location	Subject	Lunch
Miss Privy	Sports Field	Music	Caesar Salad
Mr. Head	Hall	Geography	Instant Noodles
Mr. Lav	Canteen	French	Baked Potato
Mrs. Crapper	Classroom	Maths	Ham Sandwich

The maths teacher, Mrs. Crapper, did a poo in the classroom after finishing her ham sandwich. Turns out her poo isn't in the right place after all.
"A fine example you've set the children!" Inspector Poupe comments as she is escorted from the premises. He knew something about her didn't quite add up.

MEDIUM 18

Suspects	Title	Stool Colour	Stool Shape
Augufftus	King	Chocolate	Long and Smooth
Beedlebum	Duke	Golden	Lumpy
Pottyson	Prince	Yellow	Liquefied
Thomass	Earl	Dark Brown	Round

King Augufftus left a long, smooth, chocolatey stool without deigning to flush. He usually leaves this to his butler, as well as the wiping of course.
It's not every day that Inspector Poupe apprehends a king, but nobody is above the law.

MEDIUM 19

Suspects	Occupation	Poo Preference	Match
Janey Crack	Plumber	Speckled	Tommy Twos
Kim Smellsbum	Toilet Cleaner	Curly	Paul Potty
Lucy Loo	Gastroenterologist	Shiny	Bobby Floater
Sue Idge	Sewage Worker	Dark	Keith Downunder

Gastroenterologist Lucy Loo did the poo, but is nevertheless happily engaged to the wonderful Bobby Floater! She looks forward to many shiny poos.
"Who says romance is dead?" Inspector Poupe sighs dreamily.

MEDIUM 20

Suspects	Fart Duration (seconds)	Loudness	Bouquet
Arty Farty	3.14	80 decibels	Stinky Tofu
Guffy Buffy	11.2	40 decibels	Mouldy Cheese
Ivana Dump	9.7	90 decibels	Rotten Eggs
Smelly Kelly	5	10 decibels	Sour Milk

It was Smelly Kelly, with her five-second, 10 decibel fart!
After solving the case, Inspector Poupe quickly takes his leave, gasping for breath. Even years of hardened investigation into matters scatological haven't prepared him for the grotesque stench in the room created by all those fart odours mixing together something rotten.

HARD 1

Suspects	Job title	Years at sea	Possible motive
Ann Kerr	Security Officer	4	Pay Dispute
Ash Orr	Disc Jockey	3	Dare
Cat A. Meringue	Chef	2	Drunk
Dec Hand	Croupier	1	Dislike Captain

It was Ash Orr, the disc jockey who had been at sea for three years.
"You've shown your true colours now, sonny," chuckles Poupe as he delivers Ash to the captain. Let's hope he's not made to walk the plank.

HARD 2

Suspects	Beach Location	Party Size	Windbreak Colour
The Bottoms	Sand Dunes	5	Orange
The Dumps	Damp Sand	4	Green
The Parps	Dry Sand	3	Sand
The Windies	Rock Pool	2	Brown

There were just two members of the Windies family present, but whilst it takes two to tango, it only takes one to do a poo. Realising their strategic error of sitting by the rock pool, far away from the sanctuary of the café toilets, one of the Windies decided to do more than just break wind by the brown windbreak.
"More rock poo than rock pool," Poupe chuckles to himself, as he licks on his tasty chocolate ice cream.

HARD 3

Suspects	Planet	Distance Travelled	Food
Assoroth	Krapton	100 light years	Bin Juice
Bumrox	Fartacus Minor	200 light years	Moon Cheese
Lax'tiv	Alpha Latrina	150 light years	Splatterfruit
Poozorg	Poopiter	250 light years	Space Beans

The poo was launched by Bumrox, 200 light years from Fartacus Minor after consuming a dangerous amount of moon cheese on the journey.
"BEEP BOOP ZOOORG BEEP" cried Bumrox in protest, but their objections fell on deaf ears.

HARD 4

Suspects	Toilet used	Party Colours	Election Slogan
Ben Down	Three	Brown	Flush with Success
Enni Ma	Four	Black and White	More PCs More WCs
Jimmy Riddle	Two	Yellow	Spend a Penny for Free
Mayka Puddle	One	Beige	Free Bogroll for All

It was Mayka Puddle, wearing her beige rosette, who made more than a puddle today in toilet one! Overcome with excitement at being the first person to christen the best public toilet in Looville she was too hasty and didn't realise it had a fancy transparent toilet seat. That'll teach her to pay attention to the small details.
"It's an open-and-shut case," chuckles Poupe to himself as the lady in beige turns a strange shade of red.

HARD 5

Suspects	Travel Class	Flights Taken	Aeroplane Food
Hannah Hugecrap	Business	6	Fish
Liam Letrip	Economy	1	Bottled Water
Robin Ripesmell	First	11	Porridge
Ted Takeoff	Premium Economy	16	Meat

It was Hannah Hugecrap, travelling business class, on her sixth flight!
When the smell worsens, Poupe instructs the cabin crew to make an emergency landing, the pilot passing out from the stench just seconds after the plane comes to a halt. His quick thinking has saved hundreds of lives.

HARD 6

Suspects	Vintage	Wine Type	Status
Bert Breakwind	1945	Smellion	Shitfaced
Rebecca Reeks	2020	Assti Spufarte	Sober
Sommelier Stool	1995	Pinot Marron	Tipsy
Winifred Willfart	1970	Chartdonhay	Pissed

It was Bert Breakwind, the shitfaced drunk, after drinking a 1945 Smellion!
Poupe's investigation doesn't last long, as Bert is discovered snarting (snorting and farting) in a nearby alcove. An inspection of his trousers is all that's needed to confirm his guilt.

There's about a glassful of the priceless Smellion remaining. Poupe doesn't fart around, and downs the last of the bottle. It would be a shame for it to go to waste, though it does cause Bert to whine.

HARD 7

Suspects	Subject	Degrees	Location
Dr. Sewers	Bullshit Studies	7	Lecture Hall
Lecturer Tidswiddle	History of Fart	11	Old Library
Professor Xcrement	Poolitical Sciences	5	Study
Senior Tooter	Diarrhoeal Dialectics	9	Seminar Room

It was Lecturer Tidswiddle in the old library! Reading the collection of poo jokes brought on a fascinating academic breakthrough so incredible he immediately pooed on the floor.
"You would expect better from a man with eleven degrees," remarks Inspector Poupe.

HARD 8

Suspects	Mothers	Fathers	No. of Peekaboos
Baby Badsmell	Spotty Sarah	Dunny Duncan	3
Baby Bogroll	Mucky Michelle	Longpoo Lewis	2
Baby Bottyburp	Turdy Trisha	Gross Grant	1
Baby Brownbib	Pungent Polly	Arsey Andy	4

It was Baby Badsmell, the son of Spotty Sarah and Dunny Duncan!
The other parents cast judgmental glances at the unhappy couple and the stinking child in their arms. Shortly after, the smell sets off the other babies, who begin to bawl and fill their nappies.

HARD 9

Suspects	Fruit	Job Title	Time
Dirty Dougal	Durian	Chief Stool Handler	Three Hours
Fartacious Fran	Watermelon	Head of Smell Testing	Four Hours
Odo Russ	Pineapple	Binary Translator	One Hour
Toby Turdiano	Mango	Emergency Plumber	Two Hours

It was Odo Russ, the binary translator! His pineapple-scented poop was the freshest of all, just one hour old. "Congratulations, Poupe!" his boss booms. "You solved the case faster than Robo-Poupe! Sterling work."

"Then I get to keep my job?" the inspector asks hopefully. His boss shakes his head.

"Sadly not. You see, we need to pay you a salary, while – after the original investment – Robo-Poupe works for free. In the long term, it doesn't matter if he's slower. I'm afraid you have to be terminated!"

The android lumbers towards Inspector Poupe, its eyes glowing. "No!" Poupe shouts. "No! No! NO!"

He sits up suddenly, nearly rolling out of bed. His body is dripping with sweat.

"Just a bad dream," he murmurs. Then he wrinkles his nose. There's a familiar stink coming from under the covers.

"Oh, no," Poupe moans. "I've pooed my pyjamas..."

HARD 10

Suspects	Drink	No. Of Drinks In	Role At Wedding
Filthy Frankie	Tequila	Two	Best Man
Ropey Roger	Gin and Tonic	Three	Priest
Seedy Simon	Red Wine	One	Father Of Bride
Sleazy Stew	Champagne	Four	Groom

Sleazy Stew, the groom, proudly displayed his ring for all to see after four large glasses of champagne.
"Don't worry, you can always get it annulled!" says Inspector Poupe, consoling the tearful bride.

HARD 11

Suspects	Best Joke	Style	Order On Bill
Joe Pong	What's Brown And Sticky?	Deadpan	Second
Lou Rolls	Wanna Hear My Poo Joke?	Alternative	First
Pee Wee Jones	Why Did Turd Stay Home?	Observational	Fourth
Willy Waggle	Why Was The Poo Sad?	Ventriloquist	Third

Willy Waggle, the ventriloquist, soiled himself after cracking up at his own joke about a sad poo. He was only the third (or should I say turd?) act on the bill, but the show must go on!
"You're as big a stinker as your jokes, and that's saying something!" remarks Inspector Poupe, as he douses his culprit in air freshener.

HARD 12

Suspects	Costume	Curfew	Favourite Ride
Boris Bigshits	Vampire	21:00	Helter Skelter
Christine Crapponit	Werewolf	19:00	Ferris Wheel
Patricia Poosley	Ghost	20:00	Rollercoaster
Vincent Voidbowels	Clown	22:00	Dodgems

It was Patricia Poosley, dressed as a ghost!
Her favourite ride, the rollercoaster, had already put her on edge, and the jumpscare was too much for her. She's expected home at eight, so has to quickly get changed. When her mum sees what she's done to her pristine white sheets, Patricia is grounded for sure...

HARD 13

Suspects	Favourite Stroke	Nickname	Metres Dived
Daisy Dogshit	Backstroke	Plunger	Four
Jess Justafart	Breaststroke	Sinker	Six
Murky Mike	Front Crawl	Flusher	Ten
Straining Stuart	Butterfly	Floater	Eight

It was Murky Mike, the front-crawl-favouring swimmer known as the Flusher!
Like a squid, Mike vents ink when threatened. He spews a cloud of foul fluid from his behind, attempting to muddy the water so he can swim away. The pool has to be evacuated.

HARD 14

Suspects	Show	Channel	Role
Amanda Fetor	Log Squad	3	Angry Toilet Attendant
Bud Cheeks	Good Poos Gone Bad	4	Corrupt Traffic Cop
Chad Reekster	Bottom Bandits	1	Misunderstood Teen
Julie Funk	Know Thy Enema	2	Constipated Anti-Hero

Amanda Fetor gave such a passionate performance as the angry toilet attendant that, to her shame, she soiled herself. The raw onions can't have helped. When Log Squad aired on Channel 3, many viewers complained of the stench.
In the wake of the scandal, the actress issued a public apology live on air. "I'm deeply sorry to have disappointed our viewers," she sobs. And, as the emotions swell, she feels another bowel movement coming... quick, switch off your smellivision now!

HARD 15

Suspects	Favourite Toy	Days Out of Nappies	Snack Eaten
Dottie Potty	Spaceship	28	Toast
Lottie Potty	Car	7	Carrot Sticks
Mottie Potty	Rocking Horse	21	Cereal
Scottie Potty	Bouncy Ball	14	Scrambled Eggs

It was Mottie Potty! He'd lasted three weeks without a nappy, but a vigorous ride on his rocking horse had loosened his bowels. That, combined with the full-fat milk sloshing around his cereal, had clearly tipped him over the edge, poor boy.
"Don't worry, Mottie – accidents happen," says Mrs. Potty. "Daddy still sprinkles when he tinkles, after all."

HARD 16

Suspects	Role	Food	Grog Consumed
Ava Schitt	Captain	Hard Tack	11
Grace Less	Bosun	Lemons and Limes	5
Harold Smellson	Cook	Corned Beef	14
Jack Tar	First Mate	Tinned Pilchards	8

It was Jack Tar, the first mate, after slurping eight gallons of grog!
Poupe feels confident that Jack couldn't handle his liquor, and that – combined with the laxative effects of oily fish – led to him making a mess onboard. He's unable to find any reference to what happened afterwards, although he suspects it involved a cat-o'-nine-tails.

HARD 17

Suspects	Age In Years	Breed	Location
Big Bum Betsy	3	Gassy Highland	Lily Pond
Moody Judy	4	Methane Friesian	Meadow
Mother Udders	5	Aberdeen Anguffs	Old Oak Tree
Smelly Ellie	6	Jersey Farter	Haystack

Big Bum Betsy, the three-year-old Gassy Highland, dropped the humongous cowpat while gazing at her reflection in the lily pond.
"I always thought she was a bit of a cow," remarks Farmer Piles. Inspector Poupe promptly agrees.

HARD 18

Suspect	Position	Car Model	Sponsor
Gastro Whizz	Fourth	Krappwagen	Wet Wipes Inc
Rod Flash	First	Muck Machine	Commodes And Co
Squeaky Wheels	Second	Fartmobile	Le Merdier
Turbo Turds	Third	Crease Lightning	Soggi Arce Ltd

Squeaky Wheels wrecked Le Merdier's brand image by soiling the Fartmobile's seats. To make matters worse, that wasn't the only number two on the upholstery; after all that, the racer only finished second!
"I thought I heard squeaking," says Inspector Poupe. Squeaky Wheels refuses to comment. He says nothing. Only a shrill little trump can be heard.

HARD 19

Suspects	Scent of Fart	Flat Number	Sound of Fart
Little Jimmy Ripper	Cabbage	12	Whistle
Old Mrs. Trumpton	Spam	13	Squelch
Rosie Gusts	Egg	11	Toot
Tod Trumpets	Curry	10	Squeak

Rosie Gusts from number 11 tooted out her egg-scented farts all over Graham's sofa!
"Keep your flatulence to your own flat," growls Graham territorially.

HARD 20

Suspects	Fish Type	Number of Fish	Bait
Fishy Fiona	Pike	1	Maggots
Rude Rod	Salmon	5	Earthworms
Salty Samuel	Minnow	3	Old Socks
Thomas Tackle	Carp	7	Stale Bread

It was Thomas Tackle, the rugby-playing, stale-bread-baiting fisherman!
He caught a whopping seven carp, but should have quit while he was ahead. Poupe has his photo taken next to the turd. It's one of the largest he's ever seen.